The Best *Angel* Stories 2

EDITORS OF
GUIDEPOSTS

Conari Press

This edition first published in 2016 by Conari Press an imprint of
Red Wheel/Weiser, LLC
With offices at:
65 Parker Street, Suite 7
Newburyport, MA 01950
www.redwheelweiser.com

Acknowledgments

Every attempt has been made to credit the sources of copyrighted material used in this book. If any such acknowledgment has been inadvertently omitted or miscredited, receipt of such information would be appreciated.

"Angel in a Thunderstorm" by Linda Reed as told to Sophy Burnham and "In Silent Psalmody" by Sophy Burnham originally appeared on her blog at sophywisdom.com and are reprinted with permission from Sophy Burnham. Copyright © 2012 by Sophy Burnham. All rights reserved.

"The Angel of Hope," "Christmas Feather," and "Angels in Heaven" by Lorna Byrne are reprinted with permission of Atria, a division of Simon & Schuster, Inc. from MESSAGE OF HOPE FROM THE ANGELS by Lorna Byrne. Copyright © 2012 by Lorna Byrne. All rights reserved.

"Angel to the Rescue" by Lori Hintmeister with Twila Belk and "The Man in White" by Cecil Murphey originally appeared in *Heavenly Company* by Cecil Murphey and Twila Belk and are reprinted with permission from Cecil Murphey and Twila Belk. Copyright © 2012 by Cecil Murphey and Twila Belk. All rights reserved.

"Comforted by My Angels" and "Mom's Vision of Heaven" by Crystal McVea and Alex Tresniowski are reprinted with the permission of Howard Books, a division of Simon & Schuster, Inc. from WAKING UP IN HEAVEN by Crystal McVea and Alex Tresniowski. Copyright © 2013 by Crystal McVea and Alex Tresniowski. All rights reserved.

"The Coventry Game" is used by permission of the author. Copyright © 2013 by Laraine Anne Barker. All rights reserved.

"The Englishman," "God Sent His Angels," "The Handsome Stranger," "Island of Peace," "Tow Truck Angel," and "Vision of God's Love" by Joan Wester Anderson and "Moving Train" by Virginia Blake as told to Joan Wester Anderson originally appeared on her blog at joanwanderson.com and are reprinted with permission from Joan Wester Anderson. Copyright © 2008, 2012 and 2013 by Joan Wester Anderson. All rights reserved.

I Believe in Heaven by Cecil Murphey and Twila Belk, pages 25–27 and 37–39. Copyright © 2013 by Gospel Light/Regal Books, Ventura, CA 93003. Used by permission.

"Mister Sunshine" by Pam Bostwick, "Mom, I Saw an Angel" by Guadalupe C. Casillas, "Who's Got the Wheel?" by Sherry Jones, and "Wings of Love" by Cheryl Johnston originally appeared in *True Stories of Heaven Touching Earth* by James Stuart Bell and are reprinted with permission from Bethany House Publishers, a division of Baker Publishing Group. Copyright © 2014. Used by permission.

"On a Butterfly Wing" by Eben Alexander originally appeared in the January/February 2013 issue of *Angels on Earth* magazine and is reprinted with permission from Eben Alexander, *ebenalexander.com*. Copyright © 2013 by Eben Alexander. All rights reserved.

Scripture quotations marked (KJV) are taken from *The King James Version of the Bible.*

Scripture quotations marked (NIV) are taken from *The Holy Bible, New International Version.* Copyright © 1973, 1978, 1984, 2011 by Biblica, Inc. Used by permission of Zondervan. All rights reserved worldwide. *www.zondervan.com*

Scripture quotations marked (WYC) are taken from Wycliffe Bible. Copyright © 2001 by Terence P. Noble.

Illustration on page 1 is © 2013 by Mara Cerri. All rights reserved. Illustration on page 49 is © 2013 by Richard Faust. All rights reserved. Illustration on page 89 is © 2013 by Margaret Lee/*www.i2iart.com*. All rights reserved. Illustration on page 129 is © 2013 by Raul Colon. All rights reserved. Illustration on page 173 is © 2013 by Dan Andreasen. All rights reserved. Illustration on page 201 is © 2013 by Robert Steele. All rights reserved. Illustration on page 229 is © 2013 by Anne Wertheim. All rights reserved. Illustration on page 259 is © 2013 by Greg Becker. All rights reserved.

ISBN: 978-1-57324-691-0
Library of Congress Cataloging-in-Publication Data available upon request.

Cover design by Jim Warner
Cover photograph © Nadia Strelkina licensed
Interior design by Müllerhaus
Interior art by Valerie Sokolova
Typesetting by Aptara, Inc.

Printed and bound in Canada
MAR
10 9 8 7 6 5 4 3 2 1

Contents

Chapter 2
Calling All Angels   49

Chapter 3
Angels Watching over Me   89

Chapter 4
Angels from the Realms of Glory   129

Chapter 5
Touched by an Angel   173

Chapter 6
Sleep in Heavenly Peace   **201**

SPECIAL SECTION
All Creatures Great and Small   **225**

SPECIAL SECTION
Hark! The Herald Angels Sing!   **255**

Introduction

ANGELS ARE EVERYWHERE, AND THEY are watching over us. In *The Best Angel Stories 2,* you will meet them in cities and farms, on hills and mountaintops, on roads, bridges, and in train stations. There are guardian angels bringing comfort and protection and rescuing angels performing incredible feats. You'll encounter angels appearing as white-robed beings with wings, as a bright golden light, and as extraordinary helpers appearing as humans who disappear in an instant. There are animal angels unaware and angels giving inexplicable aid to humans, restoring tender hearts through a tiny feather, snowflake, or butterfly.

As editor-in-chief of *Angels on Earth* magazine, I have shared hundreds of angel stories with our readers over many years. I can attest from these amazing stories that there is nothing like the healing touch of an angel to profoundly deepen one's faith and trust in God. Shining through the more than eighty true angel stories in this book is one of my treasured Bible verses: "Be still, and know that I am God" (Psalm 46:10, NIV). *Be still* because God's angels are ever near. *Be still* because angels answer before you call. *Be still* because angels never sleep. They keep watch all day, all night.

In this collection are the best angel stories of the year from *Angels on Earth* magazine, as well as all-new angel tales that no one has yet read. There are wondrous surprises from other sources, plus "Special Bonus! The Best Angel Stories of All Time," beloved Guideposts classics that have stood the test of time.

The mysterious and miraculous await you. A boy with a snakebite is carried home, but who helped him? Only his dog was with him. After a bad car accident, an injured woman finds herself in a field of sunlit buttercups with a comforting angel. But she was rescued in a cornfield on a rainy day. At Christmas, a grieving daughter sets up her Nativity of eleven figurines. But where did the twelfth one come from? Had her newly departed mother sent the angel to watch over her?

Again and again in these pages, you'll discover God's magnificent care: "For...He shall give his angels charge over thee, to keep thee" (Luke 4:10, KJV). Now open the doors and let the ministering angels in. Their many blessings cannot be contained! And please share your own angel story with me. Send a manuscript with a self-addressed stamped envelope to *Angels on Earth,* 110 William Street, Suite 901, New York, New York 10038 or via e-mail to submissions@angelsonearth.org.

—COLLEEN HUGHES
Angels on Earth, Editor-in-Chief

The Best Angel Stories 2

CHAPTER 1

Angels on Assignment

Death Valley Rescue

Lois Turner

TWO DAYS INTO OUR FAMILY trip to the West Coast, I was beginning to think I'd made a mistake in coming. My nephew and his wife, my two sisters and my husband had all flown two thousand miles from Batesville, Indiana, to Las Vegas to see some of the area's famous natural landmarks, particularly Death Valley in the Mojave Desert. Everything was exotic and beautiful—but dangerous too.

"It will be an adventure!" my nephew Jim had said when he originally called and asked me along for the trip. "You've never been to the West Coast, Aunt Lois. And this could be your last chance."

"You're right," I said then. Now I wondered if I should've let that chance go by. I was seventy-five, and the temperature here was in the eighties. On the floor of Death Valley it could be much hotter—I hoped the group wouldn't want to go. The landscape whooshing past the window of the van was dramatic—and unforgiving. Was this a safe place for someone my age?

"Welcome to Dante's View," Jim announced, pulling into a parking spot. "It overlooks Death Valley and the salt flats that have formed in its basin due to the extreme heat. We're fifty-five hundred feet up!"

Fifty-five hundred feet? I thought. *God, keep me safe!*

Jim parked the van and we all got out. People milled around. I didn't see anyone my age. It was a breathtaking sight: the pale valley below; mountains on all sides; a clear, blue sky overhead. But I didn't see any guardrails. My husband, John, spied a little lookout point away from the others. "Let's check out the view from there, Lois," he said.

I followed John to the lookout. We stood several feet apart, staring out at the sprawling valley below. In the grandeur of nature, I relaxed a little. I even took a few steps closer to the edge to get a better look.

My foot slipped. I heard pebbles going over the side of the mountain. There wasn't time to scream. My legs slid down the rocks. Frantically I clawed with hands and feet to get a foothold, but I kept sliding. *Dear Lord, I'm going over!*

I closed my eyes as my whole body slid several feet down the mountain until I hit something hard and solid. *A guardrail!* I thought. Using the solid metal to push off against, I scrambled back up the mountain. "John!" I cried out.

He came running. I was covered in dirt and blood from scrapes on my arms and legs.

"I'd be dead if it wasn't for that guardrail," I said.

"What guardrail?" he asked. John went over to the spot where I slipped. "There's no guardrail there, Lois. Something else stopped your fall."

I wasn't injured, just in shock. Back at the hotel John patched me up with some Band-Aids.

"I felt a guardrail," I told him.

"You felt something," he said. "But that was no guardrail. It was your guardian angel."

I was suddenly flooded with a sense of safety like I'd never known before. The rest of the trip was amazing. I didn't miss a thing. Not even the floor of Death Valley. I would go to Dante's View again, although I'd be much more careful. It will always be a special place for me, a place where I learned that life *is* one big adventure. And no matter what happens, no matter how old I get, there will always be angels to guard over me.

Stranger in the Cornfield

Nick & Kendra Leibold and Aaron Blatti

Nick Leibold:

JUST AFTER 11:00 AM AND already the sun was blistering hot in Northern Iowa. Sweat ran down my back as I finished mowing a wide strip of grass between endless rows of corn—an area with drainage too poor for crops. Not that we'd seen rain lately. The ground was dry and dusty, coating everything with a film of dirt.

Thankfully I was nearly done, just in time for lunch with my wife, Kendra. Normally I'd be inside an air-conditioned cab, but for small jobs I like driving my dad's 1963 John Deere tractor, pulling a mower behind me. I'm a fourth-generation farmer, born and raised here, like most of my neighbors. Around these parts no one is a stranger.

I backed the tractor to the edge of the field, close to a post I'd wrapped with old wire fencing taken down years ago. I heard a loud scraping noise, like the mower blades had caught on something. I pressed the control to lift the blades—

Out of nowhere, a sharp pain stabbed me in my chest. Hard to get a breath. I had to get off the tractor! But I could barely move. I half-fell, half-stumbled to the ground. Lying there on my right side, I was helpless. Didn't have the strength to grab my cell phone from my right pants pocket. *How long before Kendra comes looking for me?* She was my only hope. This time of day everyone was working.

No one would be driving down our road. It was all I could do to keep my eyes open. The sun was beating down on me. "Please hurry," I whispered. What was the point? There was no one to hear my plea.

Aaron Blatti:

"Nick, can you hear me?" My neighbor barely nodded. A circle of blood pooled on his back. Not fifteen minutes before, I'd decided to take my antique tractor for a spin. Normally I go straight at the intersection. But today I'd felt a strange urge to turn left. That's when I saw Nick lying in the grass, the mower sitting over some rusty old wire fencing nearby. Could a piece of wire have plunged into his back? It looked like he'd been shot.

"We're going to get you help," I said. I hit speed-dial on my cell phone for the sheriff's department. "Nick Leibold's been hurt bad," I said. I called my wife to call Kendra. *Dear God, please keep Nick alive, at least until his wife can get here.*

Minutes later I heard a car coming up the road. A brown van pulled in behind my tractor. The van was spotless, not a speck of dirt on it.

A white-haired man walked toward me. No one I'd ever seen before. A farmer, dressed in jeans and a button-down short-sleeved shirt, his hair neatly trimmed under a ball cap. "Anything I can do?" he asked.

"We are waiting on the ambulance," I said. "We may need help lifting him."

The man nodded. "I'll stand here and block the sun." I wouldn't forget the kindness from a complete stranger.

At last Tim Phillips, a volunteer first responder, arrived. He put an oxygen mask over Nick's face and cut the back of his shirt open, an entry wound barely visible. Kendra pulled up. "The most important thing is to keep him calm," Tim told her. But I could see the worry on his face. We were running out of time.

Kendra Leibold:

I wasn't scared. Not at first. Nick didn't seem to be in pain. There was only a little blood on his back. I crouched next to him and stroked his cheek. "I'm right here, honey," I said.

The ambulance arrived and the paramedics rushed a backboard to Nick's side. The men lifted him onto it and then each of us took a corner and carried it to the ambulance. The ambulance pulled away, roaring down the road. *Wow, they're in a hurry,* I thought, my chest suddenly tightening. *That can't be good.* I saw the almost-gleaming brown van leaving behind it.

"Did you get that farmer's name?" Aaron asked.

"No," I said. "I figured he was a friend of yours."

Aaron made me promise to call if I needed anything. "We'll be praying for you and Nick," he said.

I hopped in the car, the ambulance and the van up ahead, a thick cloud of dust billowing behind them.

At the hospital it seemed like forever before a doctor met with me. "Your husband has massive internal bleeding," he said. "He needs major surgery. We're going to airlift him to the Mayo Clinic."

An icy chill ran down my spine. Nick was dying! The Mayo Clinic was seventy miles away in Minnesota. *What if there wasn't time?*

"I'll let you know when the chopper gets here," the doctor said. "Until then, we're doing our best to keep him stable." He went through the doors, back into the ER. I wanted to see Nick. *Had I told him I loved him that morning?*

Soon Pastor Kevin arrived with Nick's dad, Joe, close behind. We waited together. At last the doctor escorted us back to Nick. He was semiconscious, an array of monitors flashing and beeping, IV tubes running from his hand. I touched his arm and kissed him. "I love you," I said. *Could he even hear me?*

"Dear God," Pastor Kevin prayed. "Help Nick and Kendra feel Your comforting presence."

I tried to feel God beside me, but all I felt was worry.

The chopper arrived for Nick, and Joe and I left for the Mayo Clinic. The drive seemed never ending. Nick seemed someplace unreachable, a world away. I tried to focus on Pastor Kevin's prayer. *God, are You really here with us?*

We found the ER and I ran inside while Joe parked the car. It was 1:30 PM. A nurse took me to a waiting room to speak with a doctor. "Your husband's in surgery," he said. "He went through three bags of plasma on the way here. Good thing the chopper had plasma on board. Not all of them do."

We sat in the waiting room for hours. I felt helpless. Friends and family drove up to be with us. I appreciated them, but all we could do was pray. It didn't seem like enough.

It was evening when the surgeon came to the waiting room. I searched his face for any sign of hope but found none. "Your husband's suffered a major trauma," he said. "We found a small piece of wire lodged in the back of his breastplate. It ruptured a major vein, the vena cava, and went through his heart, liver, and diaphragm. He's had a huge amount of internal bleeding. I'm hoping he'll make it through the night, but you need to prepare yourself…"

I felt faint. The news only seemed to get worse by the hour. Nick needed a miracle, something amazing, like the healing touch of an angel. But what were the chances of that? I needed to be realistic. That's what the surgeon was telling me.

Aaron Blatti:

The next morning I drove down mile after mile of back roads, looking for that brown van. It'd nagged at me ever since I'd come home from Nick's cornfield. I knew everyone in town, knew the cars they drove. I'd never seen that old farmer or his van. Besides, how could it not have been covered in dirt like every other car in these parts? I had to get to the bottom of it.

"I think he was an angel," my wife said plainly. But I was skeptical. Surely I'd know if there was an angel standing beside me. Still, I'd driven for hours, even stopped and asked folks if they knew of a brown van. No one had the faintest idea what I was talking about.

Kendra Leibold:

I pushed Nick in his wheelchair to the hospital chapel. A week and a half had gone by since that first fear-filled night here at the Mayo Clinic. It was only now, after two more marathon surgeries, that I dared believe that Nick was going to live.

Even the doctors were amazed. It was humbling, mind-boggling really. We knew that Nick had months of recovery ahead of him, but I couldn't wait to thank God for all that had happened. Aaron arriving in the nick of time. The stranger who had—"Honey," I said, barely able to contain my excitement. "Do you remember the farmer who stood by you?"

Nick nodded. "He blocked the sun," he said.

"Maybe he did way more than that," I said. "Aaron could never track him down. Couldn't find any proof he existed at all. Aaron's wife thinks he was an angel sent to watch over you."

Nick looked up at me from his wheelchair and smiled.

Two days later, the doctor cleared Nick to go home. "I can't explain it," he said. "But there's no longer any need for therapy." It seemed Nick's angel was still on the job, the comforting presence Pastor Kevin had asked for.

Nick Leibold:

Aaron came to visit soon after we returned home. "You're looking better than the last time I saw you," he said. The three of us talked about everything that had happened: Aaron deciding to take a joyride, his sudden urge to go by our fields, the care of the first responder, the helicopter carrying plasma, my miraculous recovery—and, of course, the unaccounted-for stranger.

It was a lot to take in. To think that we'd all been in the presence of a heavenly being, how he'd quietly seen to every detail of my care. Amazing! And yet, like a farmer, he hadn't drawn attention to himself, happy to give the glory to God, the One Who makes all things possible.

Uninvited

Renee Coy

THERE'S NOTHING LIKE RIDING THE team bus home after a big win over your rival high school. The laughter, the shouts, the highlights recalled and recounted. It was one of our track team's best victories. I don't think I ever felt closer to my teammates. I wished the night would go on forever. But up ahead was our high school parking lot, where our parents were waiting to pick us up and drive us home.

Quickly, we said our good-byes and headed toward our cars. Funny, I didn't see mine. I searched the parking lot for Mom's blue car. It wasn't anywhere. Halloween was a few days away, and a cold wind blew leaves across the lot.

One by one, the parking lot emptied. A teammate spotted me. "Do you need a ride?" she called from her parents' car.

"No, I'm okay," I said. "My mom's on her way."

The teammate smiled. "You sure?" We were good friends. At the meet that evening, I had won the mile race and she had won the 440-yard dash.

"Yeah, I'm sure," I said. She held her index finger high, signaling that we were number one. I waved good-bye. She and her mom drove off. The last thing I saw was my friend's big grin. When her car disappeared into the darkness, I was alone.

I looked at my watch: 10:45 PM. Mom was already half an hour late. I sat down on the front entrance to our high school. *You've never been this late before. In fact, you've never, ever been late.* This was long before cell phones.

I sat alone in the one pool of light, by the front entrance, for another half hour. The parking lot was dark. So was the school, except for a dim row of lights that lit the main hallway. The night was growing chilly. I pulled my team jacket around me, but it didn't give much warmth.

The street out front was pretty quiet. I could hear as cars approached. A car drove by, filled with kids, probably out cruising. A second car passed. A big, white luxury car. *Where is Mom?* I wondered. Now I was worried. *Did something happen?*

I heard a third car approach. I looked up, hoping. *Wait a minute,* I thought. *That's the same white luxury car that passed here a few minutes ago.* I heard voices, male voices I didn't recognize. *What are they doing?*

The car slowed as it passed the school. It drove up the street and then turned around and drove slowly past again. I knew they were looking at me. When they cruised beneath the streetlamp at the school entrance, I saw three grown men inside.

Keep calm, I thought. *Walk out of here. You don't want to get trapped in the dark alone.*

My cousin lived a few blocks away. When the car had rolled past, I headed to the street. As soon as I hit the sidewalk, I started to run toward her house. To my horror, the white car had turned around. It pulled up beside me. The passenger window rolled down.

"Hey, you," one of the men called. "You need a ride?"

"Leave me alone," I said. I backed off the sidewalk, trampling a line of yellow mums planted along the fence. *Maybe the people who live here will let me inside,* I thought. But the house was dark. So was every house on the street.

"Did you hear that, boys?" the man in the car cackled. "She wants to be left alone. Well, I don't think we can do that. Leave you alone."

I couldn't see what the man looked like, other than he had dark hair and a look on his face that frightened me. Before I knew it, he was out of his car, running toward me. He grabbed my jacket. I pulled loose and ran.

I was near the end of town, running down a street that ended in woods. I raced past house after house, all of them dark. The last house on the street belonged to Mr. Garrison, the high school geography teacher. He was tough as nails. But the men were back in the car, following me. Mr. Garrison was the only person on the street I knew. I didn't want to disturb him. But what choice did I have?

We lived in a quiet town, one where many people left their doors open. *God*, I prayed, *let Mr. Garrison's door be open. If I can just get inside, those men will think I live there and go away.*

I raced to his house, leaped the stairs to the porch, placed my hand on the doorknob. Closing my eyes, I turned it. The door opened. I stepped inside. Out in the street, the car sat for what seemed like a long time, then drove away.

I'm safe! Then it hit me—I was in Mr. Garrison's front hallway. I'd let myself in, uninvited. I stood there for a few minutes till I collected myself. Then I tip-toed out the door and onto the porch. The white car was gone. I ran full-speed to my cousin's house, a few blocks away. I called home, trying to locate Mom. Turns out her car had broken down in the country. She had been stranded in the dark, herself. She had been worrying about me, asking angels to keep me safe.

Back in school on Monday, I passed Mr. Garrison's classroom. He was sitting alone at his desk. I summoned all my courage and told him what had happened.

"I was home, but I was in bed," he said. "I didn't hear a thing." His brows furrowed. "And I never, ever leave my door unlocked. You couldn't have been in my house."

I repeated his house number and described some of the things in his front vestibule: an old grandfather clock, a deep-red Oriental rug, the hardwood floors. He didn't know what to say.

"My door is always locked," he said. "Always."

"I'm sure you did lock it," I said. "Just as I'm sure something heavenly opened it for me."

Light on the Red Car

Sharon Lindeman

IN THE SUMMERTIME WHEN I was growing up my family loved to camp. I was seven years old, and that year we went to Green's Lake in Southern California. It was an especially beautiful time. The fir trees blew so softly in the wind. Their pine needles scented the air. The sun on the lake slanted so that one could see tiny specks of light jumping out of the water. Everything seemed fresher and brighter up here in the mountains.

One night we were sitting around the campfire—my father and mother, brothers and sisters, and my uncle, aunt, and cousins. Most of the children were roasting marshmallows except for me. I never liked marshmallows. But I loved hot chocolate, and hot chocolate would taste good right about now, I thought to myself. I knew just where to get the water to boil for the cocoa. At the top of the nearby hill was a water faucet and I decided to make my way up there. I hopped up to get a pitcher.

The sky was dimly lit with stars and the night air was cool, perfect for having a campfire. I was off with the pitcher in hand. We kids fended for ourselves at camp, and it was nothing for me to wander about around the grounds or into the woods, or climb the hill, like now, to get water.

There were many campsites scattered all around, their campfires and lanterns glowing. In the sky there was a scattering of stars and only a sliver of a silver moon.

However, that didn't matter as I had taken my flashlight. As I skipped I thought happily of the day—how my father always made the pancakes in the morning and Mom fixed the rest of the breakfast. We kids ran around, swam in the lake, and played in the sand, listening to the lake softly lapping on the edge of the shore.

I was filled with so much excitement that I almost passed the water faucet hidden in the darkness at the top of the hill. Turning the spigot, water gushed out and filled my pitcher to the brim. I turned to go back down the hill, thinking of the hot chocolate I would soon have.

That was when it hit me. It was really dark up here, and when I looked around I saw that I was lost. Below was a sea of campsites with their own lanterns and campfires, but each one looked the same! I was all turned around and I could not remember which way I had come up the hill. Which trail should I take to go back down? Which one would lead me back to my family? I was suddenly filled with fear.

At that moment the tears just started spilling out. Everything became a wet blur. I searched and searched for the way to go. I stepped on a dirt path that led to a paved road but I wasn't sure where it would lead. Then I remembered we had a red Volkswagen van so I looked through my tears to see if I could spot it. But I still could see nothing in the inky blackness. Now I was feeling cold and very afraid on the top of the hill, uncertain what to do.

Then as if speaking to me, I saw it. A brilliant beam from the heavens like an angel of light in the night had settled on a red car below, not at all like our car but it was red. And for me, red meant hope. And this light was blinding so that it was the only thing I could see clearly—a funnel of light from the sky to the red car. I felt so comforted by the light that I just started to run, straight away down the hill toward the car. I didn't care that it wasn't our car. All I knew was that it was red and the streaming light mesmerized me so that nothing else mattered. I slid over stones, skidded on gravel. I fell and the water spilled all over me, but I just kept running to the light.

When I finally reached the red car, I saw that right across the street was my family's own red Volkswagen. And there was my family around the campfire, laughing, singing, and roasting their marshmallows. I was so filled with joy and relief. I ran to my family, soaked, and joined them as if no time had passed. But for me it felt like hours. I got up to put on dry clothes but first looked around for the brilliant guiding light and the red car that was exactly across the road from my family's car.

There was no red car. There was no beaming light. Everything was normal, campfires, lanterns, stars, and silver moon in the sky. No matter. "I will not leave you comfortless" (John 14:18, KJV). I knew the angel of light guided me home. And I've never forgotten.

AAA Means Triple Angel Coverage

Delores Topliff

When Dad turned ninety-two in Oregon, I wanted to be there. But I live in Minnesota, 1,700 miles east. I could hop a plane or train, but I hoped to see friends in Colorado, Montana, and Washington.

This grandma loves long-distance driving. I got my car serviced—good to go. My younger son insisted I buy AAA coverage—something I'd never had. For his peace of mind, I did.

The first thousand miles was uneventful. But climbing steep hills and curves to Estes Park, my car started shuddering and slowed to thirty-five miles per hour. Others sped past. Maybe it was altitude, and mine would improve going downhill. It didn't. Saturday evening in Wyoming, it slowed more, overheated, and started smoking.

Far from anywhere, fighting strong prairie winds, I pulled over and raised the hood. Radiator and oil levels were fine. I looked around. No lights or buildings were visible. There was little traffic. No one stopped. No cell phone signal. I checked my engine, prayed, and let the car cool. When I drove again and resumed cruise control, every symptom returned.

I limped into Casper. Early Sunday, a gas station attendant checked my engine. "Everything looks great. Maybe you got bad gas and it's burned out. You could stay and see our mechanic tomorrow—or keep driving."

Dad was waiting. Back on the road, I phoned a helicopter mechanic friend. "It might be your transmission. Or water in the gas or a gas line problem. An engine additive might help."

I tried everything. On level stretches, the car seemed better. I approached hills and built speed to coast up. Sometimes I made it. Others, I turned around to try again with a second run.

Where Highway 25 meets east-west I-90, a giant green highway sign pointed east toward Bismarck and Minneapolis—back home. Or west to Billings and beyond. I hesitated. "Lord, is this trip over? Do You want me to go back?"

The strong impression came: *It won't be easy, but I'll get you there.* Reaching Kalispell, Montana, that night, I'd driven three hundred miles extra to see a dear friend. After hugging hello, I said, "Please recommend a mechanic."

She frowned. "Can't. Tried them all, poor results. If I were you, I'd keep going."

I phoned my brother in Portland.

"Unless it's your transmission, nurse your car here. My mechanic, George, works miracles."

I gulped. "I'll try. Tell Dad I'm coming."

Five hundred ninety miles to go. The next day I built up momentum for the mountains, but with road construction, I missed I-90 and found myself on a narrow highway heading west. Wooded hills and gorgeous mountains paralleled the Clark Fork River. *A mistake, but so beautiful.*

My cell phone rang. I don't answer while driving, but this could be helpful. My phone was in my purse in the backseat. With my left hand holding the wheel, my right grabbed my purse. Success! Until my purse snagged on a coat hanger.

Every action still has an equal and opposite reaction. Snagging my purse pulled my car right though the road curved left. An aluminum highway marker was right in front of me. Jerking to miss it, my car crossed the median—thankfully empty of traffic. I tried to correct but couldn't straighten. My car headed toward a steep bank. Nothing helped. Angled along a steep diagonal, I would roll. "God, help!"

Suddenly, my front wheels hung up on something, pulled me straight down the slope instead of the sideways diagonal. In slow motion I plowed downhill into marshy swamp and trees, water and thick mud flying everywhere. A tree snapped off. It and brush covered my car. I stalled.

Heat shimmers rose. Angels dancing? Something or Someone had saved me from serious harm. *THANK YOU!*

My hands shook too hard to activate my cell phone. When I could manage, there was no signal. I sloshed to the front of my car to inspect the damage. Downed muddy trees blocked me. The car started, but I couldn't reverse up out of the swamp to climb the hill.

What now? I climbed to the highway. As a black Suburban sped by, I pointed downhill. The mother and daughter inside spotted my car and hit the brakes.

"What's wrong?"

"Missed a curve, overcorrected."

"You're okay?"

"Yes, but need help."

They turned around. "Hop in. The next town's four miles back."

I contacted AAA. This location, almost Idaho, was hours from their closest base. Could I arrange a local tow truck?

Yes. In Noxon, Montana, population 218, that meant Mike, a cheerful preacher, and his wife and granddaughter, who had me climb in their tow truck to drive back to the accident site. They gasped when they saw my car's location.

"Wow. Are you sure you're all right?"

"Yes. God helped me."

"For sure!"

Mike and I lifted off the broken tree and debris from my car. His wife retraced my tire tracks, shaking her head as she saw the unexplained changed direction that brought me straight down the hill instead of on the dangerous diagonal that would have made me roll. "A miracle," she said.

"Yes."

Mike drove partway downhill and positioned his truck. He placed a giant hook and chain around my axle, started his engine, and backed up, noisily winding in his chain. With an ugly sucking noise, my muddy car pulled free.

"Alleluia," Mike shouted, hopping from his truck and pumping both arms in the air.

"Alleluia," we echoed. Soon my car was back on the road facing the right direction.

"Stay overnight," his wife invited.

"Thanks, but I need to reach my dad."

"I scrubbed one spot clean on your windshield," Mike said, "but there's a car wash past town to hose off your mud."

"And off me too."

We laughed. With warm good-byes, I nursed my car on, and off I went. God's helpers, including a tow truck angel, got me to Dad on time.

My brother's mechanic replaced a burned catalytic converter—eight hundred dollars later, my car ran like new. I celebrated Dad's birthday more thankful than ever for God's grace and angelic help that keeps us safe every single day.

The Man in White

Cecil Murphey

"My stomach feels queasy," I said as I drove across the washboard-rutted road in the hot, dry season of equatorial Africa. "And I'm a little nauseated."

"You want to stop? Have me drive?" my wife, Shirley, asked.

I shook my head and said, "Whatever it is will probably pass." Instead, the queasiness increased and a light, throbbing pain added to my discomfort. I drove our yellow four-cylinder British-made Ford over the rough, red-clay roads of Kenya for almost an hour. My nausea worsened, and the pain increased.

For more than four years, our family of five had lived near Lake Victoria in a remote area of Kenya. During all that time, Shirley had battled chronic malaria, and our kids suffered from malaria and a variety of other, unexplained fevers. But I hadn't been sick even once.

About five miles from home, a wave of bile washed up into my throat. I pulled over to the side of the road. Not having time to get out, I leaned over the open window and vomited. Perspiration covered my body and my strength drained away. After a few minutes, I felt slightly better and continued to drive.

Within minutes, I was flushed as if I had a fever, but I sensed my temperature was normal. I pulled into our driveway just as a spasm of pain struck my abdomen. I slammed on the brakes, flung open the door, half-fell out of the car, and vomited again. I felt so weak that I could hardly stand up. I leaned against the side of the car until Shirley came around to support my left shoulder.

Despite her outward calmness, Shirley's eyes couldn't hide her deep concern.

"I'll be okay," I whispered.

Shirley didn't believe me. She was headmistress of a girls' dormitory of a Christian mission school. She signaled one of the teenaged girls, who raced up the winding path from the cinder-block building. Both of them held me while I slowly took one step after another. I mumbled something about the pain and couldn't figure out why I was sick. I'm one of those people who just doesn't get sick. With their help, I staggered into the house and collapsed on the sofa.

Another roiling of my intestines forced me to vomit once more. This time it was the dry heaves; I had nothing left inside my stomach. The excruciating pain increased. I'd never before felt such physical torment. The dryness of my throat and mouth made me cry out for a drink. "Water, just a little water."

"Are you sure?" my wife asked.

Too weak to talk, I nodded just as pain stabbed me and it felt as if it were ripping my entire abdomen in two.

As soon as the pain eased, Shirley held a glass to my lips. "Slowly," she said.

I sipped perhaps an ounce before a violent spasm forced me to vomit up the water.

We had arrived home about four o'clock in the afternoon after finishing a two-day seminar for church leaders. Just before Shirley and I left, we ate a large meal with them of millet, rice, and chicken.

Lying in agony, I forgot about the seminar. I hurt and the pain didn't seem to ease. For the next five hours, I lay on the sofa, unable to keep down even a sip of water. Like everyone else in that remote part of the country, we had no electricity, but we did have a kerosene-operated refrigerator. Twice Shirley put ice chips into my mouth, but both times that started a fresh attack of the dry heaves.

More than the vomiting, the intestinal pain struck every few minutes. We had no medicine except aspirin. Twice I tried to dissolve one in my mouth, but I couldn't get it down.

We prayed but I didn't get any better. Someone called the local African pastor who prayed for me, but nothing changed. I couldn't lie still and thrashed with each stabbing jolt. No position alleviated the pain, and if I moved too much, the nausea returned.

Finally, weak and unable to keep anything down, I lay quietly and prayed, "God, take away the pain. Please take away my pain." It didn't get better.

About ten o'clock I forced myself to walk into the bedroom. I didn't try to undress but fell across my side of the bed. For over an hour, I lay there as new spasms struck every few minutes. My jerking disturbed Shirley, and I'm not sure she could sleep anyway. Twice she got up and laid a damp cloth on my perspiring forehead.

I took a pillow and blanket and lay on the cement floor. "I'll be all right," I said and told her to go back to sleep.

I stifled my groans as the pains continued. By midnight, I had gotten no better. My parched throat cried out for water, but I feared the vomiting would start again.

Although nausea no longer troubled me, I felt one unrelenting spasm after another. Sharp, stabbing pains wrapped themselves around my entire abdomen and squeezed tightly for maybe half a minute and slowly diminished, only to start again.

We had no telephone and lived more than fifty miles from a tiny, inadequate clinic. A Seventh-day Adventist hospital was more than a three-hour drive, and I didn't have the strength to walk out to the car for Shirley to drive me there.

I lay on the floor, feeling each pain and trying to make no noise to keep from disturbing Shirley. Just then, a light shone into my eyes.

"Oh, God, please, please touch me," I cried out as a stronger spasm hit. The pain intensified and each wave lasted longer. "Please, God, if You care…"

The sound of footsteps told me someone was in the room. The person stopped and I looked up. Standing only a foot from me was a man wearing a white suit, but I couldn't make out his features.

The man knelt beside me and laid his hand on my abdomen. Instantly, the pain vanished.

"Thank you," I said. I lay on the floor and gave thanks to God. After a few minutes I got up and crawled into bed next to Shirley. Strange as it may sound, I felt so tired, I could think of nothing but sleep. I fell asleep without trying to figure it out.

A few minutes after six the next morning, the distant ringing of cowbells awakened me. A heavy truck lumbered down the road. Everyone else in the house was still asleep.

Aware that I felt no pain, I thought of what happened during the night. "How did the man in white get inside?" I asked. I jumped out of bed and ran to the front door and then to the back. Both were still dead-bolted.

I hadn't hallucinated, of that I was sure. In fact, hallucination would have been a simple explanation. A man in a white suit had come into my room. He had touched me and removed my pain.

I had been under God's protection, and I believe a heavenly angel touched me.

Sand Angel

Karen O'Kane

THE BEACH WAS PACKED, THE historic wooden pier in Old Orchard Beach, Maine, a huge draw for both summer tourists and residents alike on a hot July afternoon. It was a perfect day for a trip to the ocean.

Cheryl, a single mom to four-year-old daughter Chrissy, as well as her fourteen-year-old sister Michelle, maneuvered through the sand to an open spot and plunked down their gear, ready for some sun, swimming, and for Cheryl, some much-needed rest. It was exhausting being the primary caregiver.

After laying out the blanket and slathering everyone with sunscreen, Cheryl finally lay down.

"Thanks, Michelle," she said to her sister, who was taking Chrissy to the water to play. "I really appreciate you watching her for a while."

Soon after Cheryl had drifted off to sleep, Michelle was at her side. "Cheryl, I can't find Chrissy."

Cheryl woke disoriented. "Huh, what? You don't know where Chrissy is?" Bolting to her feet, her mind raced. *Chrissy? Gone? At the beach, with thousands of people?*

Immediately, she and Michelle started to wade through the throngs of people. As they bobbed around one person after another trying to get a glimpse of her, Cheryl called out Chrissy's name. Each second that passed, Cheryl's fear intensified. *How will I ever find her in a crowd this size?* she thought. *This can't be happening.*

Cheryl didn't remember praying, but suddenly, the sea of people parted and a great opening appeared. Now she could see.

Scanning the perimeter of the gap, Cheryl noticed someone—an unusually tall man. She couldn't help but notice him; his tall, erect stature stood head and shoulders above anyone else's. Clad in shorts that hung to his knees, she figured him to be in his late twenties, early thirties. Unlike the other carefree beachgoers, though, he seemed to be on a mission.

But it wasn't so much what he was wearing or how tall he was that captivated her. It was what he had sitting on his right shoulder: her daughter, Chrissy.

Cheryl watched him as he closed the distance between them. When he reached her, Cheryl thought for a moment that he would walk right by. But at the exact moment he was at her side, he lifted Chrissy off his shoulders and carefully placed her in Cheryl's arms. Continually focused straight ahead, he neither looked at Cheryl nor spoke to her.

Overcome with relief, Cheryl gripped her daughter in a tight embrace. After she had calmed a bit, she turned to thank the man. She saw the backside of him some distance off, walking away from them in the same manner as he had come. He never once looked back, never deviated from his mission. Just walked off as if nothing had happened.

Back at the blanket, Cheryl marveled at what she had just experienced. *Who was that guy, a man who never directly looked at her, a man who never spoke to her, never asked if Chrissy belonged to her? And the way he acted, how odd was that?*

What struck her most, though, was the unwavering decisiveness of his actions. He was not hesitant in any way. He knew where he was going and what he was doing. He didn't waver to the left or to the right, but kept his eye on the task at hand.

"He followed God's instruction to the letter," Cheryl said later. It was a message she took to heart. Trust God with a steadfast heart. If He asks something of you, do it at once, and always, always keep your eyes focused on Him.

"He was an angel," Cheryl said to Michelle and little Chrissy the following day. "That man was an angel. How about that? An ordinary day at the beach, turned—*heavenly*."

Extra Help

Pat Waldron

IT WAS 5:00 AM. TIME to get up. I run our family's 150-year-old farm pretty much on my own, so I had to get up early to get a day's work done. Feed the animals. Check to see that all are healthy. Then to church, since it was a Sunday.

Helping hands, I thought, seated in my pew. *So much to do. If You can hear me up there, Lord, I sure could use some help.*

Following church, I hurried home and wolfed down breakfast. The farm is 188 acres. I grow wheat, soybeans, corn, and alfalfa hay, and today was the day to start the harvest. "I'm going to do the soybeans today," I told my wife, Susan, pulling on my coveralls and heading out the door. I climbed aboard the combine and drove to the fields. It was a nice day, about fifty degrees, unseasonably warm. I finished one five-acre field and motored toward an adjoining field.

That's when I heard a banging sound. *What's that?* I shut the machine off.

I hopped down to the ground and set the safety lock on the header. The header is fifteen feet wide, and looks like a giant snowblower. It cuts the soybeans, separates the beans from the pods, and then deposits them in the bin inside the combine. The lock would keep it in the raised position. By now there was smoke. A bearing had burned out, destroying the pulley. *Just my luck*, I thought. *One more thing for me to take care of.* I hiked the mile back to the barn, fetched some tools and a new bearing, and returned to fix the problem right there in the field.

Better make sure it's 100 percent, I thought. I turned on the engine, then the combine, and did a thorough visual inspection. Everything looked fine. I climbed back into the combine, ready to go. I moved a lever to let the header down, but it barely budged. *Darn, I left the safety lock on.* In a hurry now, I hopped off the machine without shutting it down.

In front of the safety lock was a spinning belt, attached to a pulley. *I'll just reach in between the belt.*

Carefully, I threaded in my left hand, freed the lock, and began to pull my hand back from behind the belt. *Slowly,* I cautioned myself, *slowly.* I was just about free when I felt a tug on my shoulder. Before I could react, I knew I was in trouble. *My coveralls sleeve! It was caught in the shaft!*

Pull, I told myself. Too late. Next thing I knew, my hand was wrapped like a pretzel around the shaft. The pulley was reeling me in! It wanted to suck me into the combine, like a soybean stalk. My head slammed against the header. My legs were pulled flush against the machinery as the spinning shaft started burning the skin from my thighs. I couldn't hold out forever.

The nearest help was a mile away. Susan wouldn't even think to look for me for hours. *I'm going to die*, I thought. I remembered what I'd prayed for in church that morning: *helping hands.* But there was only me out here. And there was only one way to save myself. *You have to pull your hand off*, I told myself. *You have to sacrifice your hand.*

I took my right hand, placed it on my left bicep, pressed my head against the header for extra leverage, and pulled. The pulley was relentless. It kept sucking me in. I could barely breathe. "God, help me!" I yelled.

I felt something pull free. There, spinning in the shaft, was my hand.

Saved, I thought, too much in shock to think about my severed limb. But I wasn't. My coveralls were still caught in the shaft, which was spinning around, pulling me in tighter and tighter like a tourniquet, squeezing the life out of me. The pulley kept reeling it in. "God, help me!" I yelled again.

I gritted my teeth. With my good arm and what was left of my other one, I pressed my head against the header once more and pushed as hard as I could. As I did, the strangest feeling came over me. I was sure someone was standing directly behind me, hands on my shoulders, helping pull me out. I swiveled my head, trying to see who it was. But no one was there. The smell of smoke grew stronger. The belt and my coveralls were burning together. The pulley kept pulling me in. *I'm almost out of time*, I told myself. I braced myself for one last effort.

There they are again, I thought. *Those hands on my shoulders, this time even stronger.* The smoke and its acrid smell grew worse. The smoke was so thick it burned my eyes until I could barely see. The invisible hands kept pulling. And then, somehow, I was free. Completely free!

I stared down at myself. Blood dripped from my arm. I was all but naked. The shaft and pulley had ripped off and eaten my clothes. I climbed into the cab of the combine and shut it down. I grabbed an old sweatshirt sitting there and wrapped it around me.

There was a country road not too far away. I lurched toward it, crossing the soybean field. But there was no traffic in either direction. I walked nearly a mile before spotting my cousin, who lives down the road from my farm. "I need help!" I cried.

My cousin phoned 911. When the EMTs arrived, I'd lost so much blood they couldn't get a pulse. A helicopter flew me to a trauma hospital in Syracuse, thirty miles away.

I was in the hospital a week. Three weeks later I was back to feeding my animals. My neighbors pitched in and finished the harvesting with their combines. I was working again, planting crops. Three months later I was fitted with a prosthetic hand.

"You have a guardian angel looking after you, for sure," Susan said the first day I came in from working the fields.

"I know I do. Probably more than one," I said.

I still take care of the farm. I do everything I used to do. I just do it differently now, knowing I'm not doing it alone. There's always an extra pair of hands helping me.

Angel to the Rescue

Lori Hintermeister with Twila Belk

A POINT OF GRACE CONCERT was a delightful way to end a fun day at the Iowa State Fair. My sister Connie and I, along with our ten-year-old daughters, made the three-hour trip early that morning so we could enjoy a full day of attractions, rides, fried food, and gazing at the famous cow sculpture made of butter.

The hot, sunny weather, typical for Iowa in August, made our day even better. We left the fair tired but content at about eleven that night.

It was sprinkling when we left and soon rain fell steadily. Heavy rains developed into a thunderstorm shortly after we began our trip home, yet our mood remained light as we belted out tunes from the concert and listened to the girls' excited chatter in the backseat of the van.

Thirty minutes into the trip, the van started to wobble and vibrate. Connie pulled onto the side of the highway. "I think we have a flat."

"What are we going to do?" I watched the rain pelt the windshield. "Do you know how to fix a flat?"

The van quivered as an eighteen-wheeler whizzed by, a reminder that we were a few feet from Interstate 80.

"I don't have any idea where the spare and jack are stored. I didn't expect problems with a new van," Connie said.

We considered our predicament. Flat tire. No cell phones. Pouring rain. No nearby buildings. Two young girls in the backseat. Pitch-black, except for the occasional flash of lightning and the lights in our van. Sparse traffic other than the semis zooming past us on the interstate. "What are we going to do?" I asked again, this time an octave higher and a decibel louder.

"I don't know."

Connie and I stepped outside the van, hoping a plan would come to us as we opened the back of the van and searched for the spare tire.

A man walked toward us. He seemed oblivious to the rain. "Where'd he come from?" Connie asked in a hushed voice.

"I don't know." For miles, we hadn't seen car headlights in front of us or behind us. Our van was the only vehicle on the side of the road.

"Can I help you?" the man asked when he came close.

I can't explain it, but something about his pleasant voice, and perhaps the way he walked, made me feel safe. He wore a white T-shirt and was probably in his late twenties.

"We need help," I said. "We have a flat tire—"

"But we don't know where the spare tire is," Connie said.

"That's okay. I'm familiar with this van." He smiled and said, "Don't worry. I know where things are, and I can take care of it."

I thought it strange that he would know about this van, especially since it was new, but I didn't argue.

Despite the rain, he changed the tire and put the flat one in the back of the van. "Is there anything else I can do for you?" he asked.

"No, we're fine now." Connie opened the driver's side door, scrambled to find her purse, and pulled out a twenty-dollar bill. "Thank you so much for your help." She held out the money.

"That's all right. Glad to do it."

Connie insisted, but he shook his head. "If there's nothing else I can do, and you're sure you're okay, I'll be on my way." He waved and walked back the way he had come, from behind our van.

We yelled good-bye and thanked him several more times. Then I could no longer see him. "He seems to have disappeared as quickly as he appeared," I said.

"He can't just walk in this horrible rain," Connie said. "But I didn't see any headlights or taillights."

"I didn't hear a door open or close," I said.

Where did he go? Did that really just happen? Who was he?

Just then I thought about our girls. We hadn't heard a word from them. "Do you think they're scared?" I whispered.

"I don't know," Connie said. "And how can we possibly explain to them what to us is unexplainable?"

Connie and I slid into the van and tried to control the shivers from our soaked clothes. We turned to face our daughters.

"Amanda? Darcy?" I asked. "Are you two doing okay?"

The girls sat quietly in the back. They were surprisingly calm.

"Yes, Mom." Amanda's voice sounded peaceful. "We're fine."

"Did you see what happened?" Connie said. "A man came out of nowhere and—"

"Amanda and I were freaking out when the van started shaking," Darcy said, "and when the thunder crashed—"

"That made it even worse," Amanda said, "and I was afraid."

"Amanda said we should pray and God would take care of us. That's what we did."

Connie and I had been so caught up in what was going on that we hadn't thought to pray.

"We prayed that God would keep us safe," Amanda said.

"We needed help, so we asked God to send someone," Darcy said. "God sent that nice man."

"We knew God would take care of us."

"God sent an angel to help us," Darcy said.

Connie and I marveled at the innocent faith of our young daughters. As we drove along, I kept rethinking that event, and spontaneously thanked God for caring and taking care of us, even though I hadn't asked.

That August night, we learned an important lesson. As Christians, we knew God was with us, but until that incident I didn't realize how easily the Lord answers our prayers. As we drove on home, I kept thinking of a verse I had known for years, but now it took on relevance: "Don't worry about anything; instead, pray about everything. Tell God what you need, and thank him for all he has done" (Philippians 4:6, NLT).

Our daughters grasped the lesson before we did.

As we understood later, it took an angel to convince us.

Who's Got the Wheel?

Sherry Jones

DRIVING HOME ONE DAY, I spotted a billboard that read, "If Jesus is your co-pilot, you'd better switch seats." That sign was just another comforting confirmation of God's constant guidance in our lives.

My husband, Randy, and I had been missionaries in Cameroon, Africa. He and his team of national translators finished translating the New Testament into the Kom language, and our task seemed finished. God directed our steps back to the United States and to a little town in Churchill, Montana.

After a few months of looking for work and finding nothing, I began to wonder if we were in the right place. I not only wondered, I worried. Had God forgotten about us? It was in October 2006 that a local potato farmer approached Randy about some work during the harvest season. Randy was all too grateful to earn a little money.

After the first day on the job, Randy quickly realized that hard work and quick wits were key ingredients to the job. Even his small position required observant eyes if things were to run well. Randy was entrusted with the task of helping unload the trucks swollen with fresh potatoes from the field onto a conveyer belt. He, along with others, had the job of separating rocks and large dirt clods from the flood of potatoes that poured onto the belt called a "stinger." From there, the fresh potatoes were carried to other stations for storing. The rocks and dirt clods were tossed into a large bucket attached to a bulldozer parked directly behind Randy's station.

Every morning Randy was up early, worked all day in cold, and rain, and heat with the others at the stinger, arriving home after dark, covered with dirt and fatigue.

One morning, just after Randy drove away to the farm, I felt compelled to pray. I called the children together. "Daddy's looking awfully tired this morning. We need to pray for him, for strength and for protection. He's working with a lot of dangerous equipment," I explained.

Randy arrived on the scene that brisk October morning as a glowing orange sun settled on the horizon. A driver backed a potato truck that had been loaded with field potatoes from the previous day, to the conveyer belt to dump its cargo. Randy and his partner took their places at the stinger, zipped up their jackets, and slid their chilled fingers into worn gloves. They dug into the mountain of spuds the moment the mound poured off the back of the truck and rumbled and bumped past their stiff fingers. Some fifteen yards away, another truck of potatoes was parked into place for the next unloading. The driver parked the truck, turned off the engine, and stepped away to work at another position.

The routine of the morning progressed as usual. Above the roar of the machinery, Randy talked and joked with his partner while tossing aside rocks and clods over his shoulder into the bucket attached to the bulldozer directly behind him. But Randy noticed that his colleague had suddenly stopped responding to him. Randy glanced up. His coworker's eyes were growing wider by the moment. His mouth had fallen open as if he wanted to say something but went suddenly mute.

Something seemed very wrong. Randy swallowed his questions and watched his partner step backward from the stinger with his eyes steadily fixed on something behind him.

Randy turned around then froze. Had he been warned ahead of time, he might have been able to jump out of the way. But it was too late. The parked truck, still loaded with a ton of potatoes, was rolling down the slope directly toward the bulldozer that rested directly behind Randy—and it was gaining speed. In a split second, Randy realized there was no escape. Once the truck hit the bulldozer, it would pin him between the bucket of rocks in front and the stinger behind, crushing him if not killing him. No time to think. No time to react. There was only one possible solution: Someone needed to be in that truck to stop it. But there was no driver.

Randy watched the unmanned truck race toward him as if everything suddenly went into slow motion. His mind was calculating the impact; his body stiffened for the jolt. Then, just before the truck collided into the bulldozer, a remarkable thing happened. The truck suddenly veered. The swerve appeared so abrupt that Randy looked up to see who had suddenly commandeered the truck. By inches, the truck missed the bulldozer. Randy watched it roll past and collide with another truck. An echo of metal against metal clanged like a loud cymbal. Everyone looked up. A collective gasp hung in the crisp morning air. The truck was driverless.

Every worker stood in place, not moving for moments. What they had witnessed was nothing short of a miracle, and many praised God for Randy's protection. With a slight turning of the wheel at the precise time, God spared Randy's life. But who turned the wheel? Did the truck turn on its own power? Or, perhaps, was there an angel of mercy in the driver's seat?

When Randy came home that night and told us what happened, we sat amazed. That incident did indeed remind us of God's power to answer prayer. It also reminded me of God's graciousness to teach us necessary lessons. Already I had been fretting about how God would take care of us, but this runaway-truck episode was a timely lesson of God's providence in our lives. God's message rang in my mind loud and clear. He was in control. He obviously had a plan for Randy's future in little Churchill, Montana. We needed to trust Him to work it out. A few months later, God's plan became evident. In the small town next to Churchill, Randy was invited to become the next pastor at Manhattan Bible Church. I was so glad God was in the driver's seat and steering our future to the exact location He wanted to put us—for His glory and our good.

Flash Flood

Priscilla Oman

IT HAD BEEN AN UNUSUALLY wet June. The morning of the sixteenth it was drizzling, but the weatherman had predicted just showers, so we had no reason to expect anything more than an ordinary rainy day.

My husband, Reuben, and I were driving from Denver to our home in Castle Rock, Colorado. We were still a bit somber and saddened for we had gone to Denver for my brother's funeral. Increasingly heavy rain seemed to darken our spirits even more.

Driving south on Highway 85, visibility became poor and the steady accumulation of water on the road made for slow driving. Soon we realized this was not an ordinary rainstorm. A fierce wind—now seeming almost at the intensity of a tornado—began pushing our car back and forth along the highway.

I gripped the car door as rocks washed onto the road, making things even more treacherous. It was taking all of Reuben's skill as a driver to keep from hitting the rocks, some of which were as large as washtubs.

As we crept along, the water rose and soon was up to our hubcaps. Ahead of us, cars began sliding off the road one by one, ending up stuck in the sand on the road shoulder. Afraid of stalling, we kept going. Suddenly a huge wall of water came crashing down upon us from the hills beside the road. Reuben and I looked at each other in terror as the car was lifted up and swept backward. Turning quickly, I could see Plum Creek—usually a mild, meandering stream, but now a roaring, torrential mudflow—directly behind us.

"Reuben," I screamed above the roar of the water, "we're going into the flood!"

He clutched my hand and together we murmured a prayer as we prepared to face certain drowning. As we braced ourselves, our car came to a sudden halt.

Looking back, I could see we had rammed into a telephone pole only a few feet in front of the raging creek. I breathed a sigh of relief and we started to get out of the car. But the doors wouldn't open! The car had sunk so far into the sand that the doors were jammed. I gasped as I looked down—our legs were caught, too, pinned in the sand that was rapidly filling the inside of the car.

Terrified and helpless, Reuben and I could only sit there and let the sand pack us firmly to our waists. Meanwhile the water both outside and inside the car rose higher and higher. There was no use shouting for help; the roaring of the flood muffled everything.

As darkness set in—the blackest night I'd ever seen—the freezing air made Reuben and me shiver uncontrollably. With the lower parts of our bodies locked tight in the sand, the water continued to creep up to our necks. We held our heads as high as possible and tilted our noses back above the water. Although I tried to keep my lips tightly closed, I found myself swallowing some of the muddy slime. "Oh, God," I prayed, "please help us. Please!"

Incredibly, just as all seemed lost, the water level began to drop and the noise of the flood seemed to lessen, as well. A sense of calm came over us. But then another problem presented itself, adding to our difficulties. In our tightly sealed prison, our oxygen was now nearly gone and the door handles were buried in wet sand. Reuben and I searched for some kind of tool to break a window, but we couldn't find anything. And time was running out for us.

In that moment of complete isolation, we knew we were probably going to die. "I guess this is it," I told Reuben.

"Yes," he answered. "But we've had a good life together."

God has given us a good life, I thought. But He had always given us courage too. Courage to fight and not give up. I thought of the forty-sixth Psalm, a favorite of mine. It said something about courage, didn't it? I began to say it out loud from memory. "God is our refuge and strength, a very present help in trouble. Therefore will not we fear, though the earth be removed, and though the mountains be carried into the midst of the sea" (verses 1–2, KJV).

The words sounded so appropriate that I began repeating them, and as I did, I felt a kind of Presence enter the car, a Presence that seemed once again to remove our fear.

Just seconds later a small stone shattered the windshield. Large rocks had been hitting the car all through our ordeal—fortunately for us, not breaking the glass at the peak of the flood, which would have drowned us. Now the small stone made a hole, not a big one, but large enough to give us breath and hope.

A few minutes later we heard voices. Being virtually buried alive, we couldn't tell where they were coming from. Through chattering teeth, Reuben joined me as I again said the forty-sixth Psalm. Was something about to happen?

I don't know what a guardian angel looks like, but when a man suddenly peered into our car, he surely seemed heaven-sent. Seeing our situation, the man ran for help and the next thing we knew a winch was being hooked to the front of our car. A grinding noise followed as our car top was pulled back like a can of sardines. Two men—one of them our "angel"—climbed into the car and carefully dug us out with shovels, then took us to the hospital in Englewood, Colorado.

At the hospital we were washed repeatedly, given warm blankets, hot tea, and told that eastern Colorado had been hit by the worst flood in its history. The hospital was filled with injured people.

The next morning we awoke without any bad effects, and as soon as the road was opened, we returned to Castle Rock. For a week afterward, though not ill, I went about my household duties in a sort of daze. Finally one morning I came out of it.

"Reuben," I said, "it's time for us to go and buy a new car."

He chuckled. "I was just waiting for you to wake up."

I put on my raincoat, the one I had worn in the flood. Sticking my hand into the pocket, I felt something. I pulled out a stem with two leaves and a tiny perfect white flower. How did it get there? Could that filthy floodwater have washed it into my pocket? It seemed so strange.

My thoughts flashed back to that day. The telephone pole in just the right place; the huge rocks that hit our windshield without breaking it; the very small stone that broke the glass to give us needed air; the water at our nose level receding just in time; and finally that man, our "guardian angel," who came at the crucial moment.

Were those events just a long line of coincidences? I looked down at the little flower in my hand—and I knew they weren't. The events were miracles, God's miracles. He had been with us all along. He had given us strength and refuge when we needed it, and He had given us the biggest miracle of all—courage to face death itself without being afraid.

Moving Train

Virginia Blake as told to Joan Wester Anderson

WHEN I WAS IN MY twenties, I had three little girls, and one on the way. I had gone to visit my mother, and stayed until midafternoon. By the time I decided to leave, however, the sky was darkening. Rain was definitely on the way.

Should I stay or go? This was only to have been a brief visit, so I had very few baby supplies with me, and I could be home via the country road within an hour.... Taking a deep breath, I buckled up my daughters and set out. It wasn't too bad in the beginning. Thunder, lightning, and a medium downpour...But as I drove, the sky got darker, and the rain denser. Eventually, the downpour was so heavy that I could not see my own hood! Terrified, I rolled down the window, trying to see the road, but I still couldn't see anything. Visibility was zero. Would another driver hit me?

I knew vaguely where I was, and my fear deepened. There was nowhere to pull over, given the deep ditches along the road, and the dense forest beyond. But worst of all, a railroad crossing was somewhere up ahead. There was only a sign posted on the crossing, not a signal, because I was way out in the boonies. No one would be able to see the warning sign until they were upon it. And then it might be too late.

My daughters had fallen asleep. It would be too difficult to awaken all three and get them out of the car, in case they could somehow run to safety.... Possible solutions flew through my mind as I continued to inch along, the rain still coming like a flood. I prayed for direction, for safety, for my vulnerable unborn baby…and suddenly the car stopped.

Wait! I hadn't touched the brake. Was the engine flooded? Then, to my utter amazement, the mist cleared for a moment. Ahead of me, no more than an arm's length from my bumper, was a moving train!

I sat for a moment, dazed, as the freight cars went by. It took some time for the train to completely pass, and when it did, I was able to see a little bit better. The storm was quieting. My family was safe. And my car started immediately.

To this day I still believe that God sent His angel to be with us. There is no way I could have stopped in time if not for the power of God.

The Widow Maker

Tim Shirk

As THE BIG YELLOW BUS wound its way up the mountain road to the camp where I would be volunteering as counselor for a group of eighth graders, I was just glad to have a week off from my senior studies at a Colorado Springs high school. Ropes courses, sports competitions, and nature hikes didn't sound too bad either.

The sun was burning off the morning dew when another counselor, Courtney, and I lined up our ten boys and ten girls for a two-hour trek through the woods near Florissant, Colorado. Having a flair for the theatrical—and to keep order in the ranks—we staged our hike along a reconnaissance theme.

I gave the "Forward march!" and we were off—halting, crouching, checking for trip wires, and sending smaller units ahead to confirm clear passage. As we cut along a small hill on trails that crisscrossed old growth forest, the campers trooped side by side in a "left right, left right" cadence. I was leading the pack.

Maybe it was the methodical tromp of our feet—or the semiserious mood of being on "red alert"—but suddenly I had the sensation that someone was coming up on us from a hidden vantage point. I tensed and looked around. I saw nothing…until I looked up.

Falling silently straight toward me was a tall evergreen tree stripped of its branches. It seemed to move in slow motion, yet it was nearly on top of me before I could react.

I pushed the kids nearest me out of the way—while instinctively bending forward and locking my hands over my head. The middle of the log landed right across my back. I felt the weight and density of the collision. A surge of adrenaline shot through me. I leapt up shouting to the others, "RUN!"

The log swiveled across my back and rolled twenty feet down the hill. I bolted up the trail. We all gathered about fifteen yards ahead. A visibly shaken Courtney—who'd been at the rear of the line, maybe thirty feet from the incident—stared at me in bewilderment. "What just happened? Are you okay? That tree landed right on you!"

I was absolutely fine. I pulled up my shirt. Not a scratch.

We crept down to the fallen tree and sized it up. It was as tall and dense as it had seemed…as difficult to move as I imagined a telephone pole would be.

Subdued, we wrapped up the hike early. At lunch Courtney told the camp director what had taken place. A worried look came over him. "You were really lucky," he said to me. "We call those 'widow makers.' They fall silently and crush whatever's in their path. Seems like we lose someone in the state every year."

I didn't think luck had anything to do with it. Had an angel slipped between my back and the falling log to absorb the blow? Or had God given me the strength of an angel to momentarily withstand what my body could not?

I walked off alone to think about it. A "widow maker" could have done me in before I'd even had a chance to marry and have children. And all else I hoped for might have vanished beneath that deadly tree. I thought beyond these things to God's design for my life—to what He was preparing me to do. From an early age

I'd believed He was actively involved with me. It was clear He had intervened to keep me from becoming another Colorado statistic.

On the way up the mountain, I was pumped to have a week free from classes and homework and regular routine. I came down a different person. I had experienced a miracle. I couldn't wait to get back in my life—to forward march into whatever future God had planned for me.

CHAPTER 2

Calling All Angels

The Sliding Door

Theresa Leaming

THE KIDS LOVED THE PLAYGROUND. My seven-year-old and five-year-old took turns careening down the twisty slide, my three-year-old tottered across the wobble bridge, and my one-year-old giggled as I pushed her in the bucket swing. Normally keeping an eye on four kids was tough, but we were the only ones at the Salina, Kansas, city park on such a dreary winter day.

A cold drop landed on my head. Soon it was drizzling. "Okay, kids, time to go!" I ushered them to our aging Volkswagen bus, unlocked it, and opened the sliding door.

The door slipped its track. It fell off and slammed down on the wet asphalt.

I couldn't drive without a door! How long would we be stuck here? There wasn't a soul in sight, and I had no way to contact anyone. *Lord, what do I do?*

A voice startled me. "Looks like it's time for a new van."

The man had appeared out of nowhere. Instinctively I stood in front of the kids. The stranger laughed. "Ma'am, I'm here to help," he said. "Let me fix that door." In a minute, he got the door back into place. He tested it. "All good now," he said.

My one-year-old bolted toward the swings. "Hey!" I shouted. I ran and scooped her up before she got far. Then I turned back to thank the stranger. He was gone.

Was he an angel? When we finally retired the bus several years later, only one part was still working. That sliding door.

A Blessing from China

Stacie Chambers

TWENTY-PLUS HOURS ON A PLANE would make anyone fidgety, but this was the most important trip of my life. My husband, Doug, and I were on our way to China to meet our new daughter and take her home to Kansas.

I pulled a handful of photos out of my purse. I had already given her a name: Hannah. She was two years old—older than many adoptees because Chinese authorities considered Doug and me too young to take an infant out of the country. To increase our chances for success—full adoption—we were open to caring for special needs. We just wanted a child! For months I'd held on to this paltry collection of pictures, wishing I could hold the little girl in them. She was a tiny thing with big brown eyes and curling wisps of dark hair. I reread for the hundredth time the brief paragraph of information the orphanage had sent. "The baby was born in the village of Wuzhou and has no family," it said. She had no family in China, but she had me. I already loved her, and I longed to know more about her. She appeared to be healthy, but I worried about her first two years. Her first smile, her first word, her first steps. Had she ever been sick with no one to comfort her? Had she cried too many tears, even for an infant? There was so much I would never know, and Hannah would never be able to tell me. I closed my eyes and prayed the prayer I'd been praying since the agency matched us up: *God, send Hannah an angel to watch over her until I get there. She's all alone in the world.*

"Almost there," Doug said. It was hard to believe our journey was almost over. We'd started trying to have children a few years before. When it didn't happen I had some fertility treatments. "It comes down to this," I said to Doug when that didn't work. "Do we want to be parents or do we want to be pregnant?"

A TV report about poor conditions for little girls in Chinese orphanages had sealed the deal for us. What could I do now but trust God to care for Hannah until we could?

Above my head the Fasten Seat Belt sign chimed. We were beginning our descent into Hong Kong. From there Doug and I and the other new parents would go on to China. "We'll arrive as a couple," Doug said. "We'll leave as a family."

It seemed like forever before we got to our base hotel in Nanning. A representative escorted the group to a building where we would meet our children. An interpreter explained the procedure. Every few minutes someone would shout out the name of a baby and a couple would make their way out of the crowd.

Finally our Hannah! Doug put his arm around me and we followed the interpreter to a little room. As if by some fairy-tale magic, there she was, so small and delicate. Our daughter! I loved her even more. "She has traveled ten hours on a bus from her village of Wuzhou," the interpreter explained. "She's tired. Give her time to rest." Hannah cried most of the way back to the hotel, but Doug and I had never been happier.

Back in our room, I rocked Hannah to sleep in my arms, wondering if she'd ever been rocked before, if she'd ever been loved. But of course I knew she had no family, and the orphanage was full of hundreds of children to be cared for. No one child could possibly stand out for special attention. *You're not alone anymore,* I thought. *You'll never be alone again.*

In the coming days Doug and I took a bus back to Hannah's village, where a notary officially released Hannah to us. That done, we prepared to take a ferry ride on the Pearl River to Guangzhou for a health report. The red tape seemed endless, and with each step I feared something might go wrong. "I won't relax until we're all back in Kansas," I told Doug as we packed our bags. *Back where Hannah has me to watch over her. Someone who loves her.*

There was a knock. I jumped. Doug opened the door. "I have someone here," the interpreter said hesitantly. "She wants to say good-bye to Hannah."

Doug and I looked at each other. I reached for Hannah. "Someone from the orphanage?" I asked.

"No," the interpreter said. "Just a friend." I took Hannah in my arms and held her tight. Doug and I followed the interpreter down the hall to the lobby. As we turned the corner, a young Chinese woman stood up. She was about my age, very pretty, with long, shiny hair. When she saw Hannah, her face lit up and she stretched out her arms. Hannah lay quietly against me as the young woman patted her back.

Hannah's not afraid of her, I thought. *She can't be a stranger. But who is she?*

The woman spoke softly to Hannah in Chinese, pausing occasionally to wipe away a tear. After a few minutes she said something to the interpreter. "She'd like to keep in touch with you," the interpreter said.

We exchanged addresses, but I was afraid to press for details. We said good-bye and gathered our luggage for the final leg of our journey. The three of us returned to Kansas as a family, just as Doug predicted. Hannah had a lot to get used to in America. But little by little she made herself at home.

One day, a few months after our return, I received a letter. "It's from the woman we met at the hotel," I told Doug as I looked it over. "There's a translation in English, and—oh, Doug, look at this!"

My hands trembled as I flipped through the packet of photos from the envelope: Hannah as an infant in her crib, Hannah hugging a stuffed animal, Hannah playing in the park, Hannah in the young woman's arms, grinning from ear to ear. The life I saw in these pictures was nothing like the lonely world I'd imagined for Hannah in the orphanage. *These are the memories she carried with her from China*, I thought. *This was what Hannah was doing while I prayed for her.*

"I don't understand. How is this possible?" asked Doug.

I read the letter out loud: The Chinese government had declared the year Hannah was born "The Year of the Family." The young woman, MoBin, wanted to do something to honor that, so she volunteered to visit the children at a local orphanage. "Among the children in Wuzhou Welfare Yard, I was attracted by a baby lying on a bed," MoBin wrote. "Her intelligent large eyes and curly hair were so lovely that I liked her at the first sight."

But Hannah was very sick. The staff didn't have much hope she would survive. MoBin begged permission to take her to a doctor. For six months MoBin cared for Hannah at her own home and returned her to the orphanage strong and healthy. MoBin continued to visit her, taking Hannah home with her on the weekends. "I called myself her auntie MoBin," she wrote. It broke her heart to say good-bye to Hannah, but MoBin was happy Hannah would have a family of her own to love her.

Doug and I would be eternally grateful to this selfless young woman. She was an answer to my prayer, an angel for Hannah on earth.

Fireman Jim

Douglas Scott Clark

KNOXVILLE, TENNESSEE, LOOKED TO BE all crowded streets, tall buildings, and smoggy air. It was nothing like home in the Smoky Mountains. But that year of 1949 when I was seven Mama and Dad had brought all us kids to the city so Dad could take a job as a machinist at a tool and die shop.

One chilly afternoon my brother, Buddy Earl, and I walked along the railroad tracks near our rented house. I carried an empty bucket that bumped against my knees as I walked. "See any coal on the ground?" I called.

"Not yet," Buddy Earl called back.

At this part of the track there was a railway crossing, and the train always slowed down here at the intersection. If we were lucky, bits of coal fell off the train and onto the ground where we could gather them up. A lot of the coal wasn't the best quality, most of it clinkers and burned-up lumps, but we needed everything we could get to keep warm.

Things hadn't gone so well since we came to Knoxville. Flatlanders—that's what we called the folks in the city—thought we were pretty strange. They had a name for us too: hillbillies. Just last week in school I'd gotten laughed at for telling the time. "It's nigh on one o'clock," I'd said.

The other kids laughed. "Nigh on one o'clock?" they repeated. "You talk funny."

I kicked some pebbles by the train tracks and frowned at the ground. I wasn't ashamed at being a hillbilly. I loved our little house on the mountain. We grew our own food in the gardens, the stream was full of fish for catching, and the woods were full of game. Here in the city you needed money for food, and money was hard to come by. Dad had come down with pneumonia, probably because our house here was so cold. You could throw a cat through the cracks in our walls, they were so big.

"Train's coming!" Buddy Earl shouted.

We stepped back from the tracks. The train slowed to a stop. Coal rattled down over the sides to the ground. Buddy and I dove to get it.

"Why are you boys digging in the snow?" someone called from the engine cab. It was a fireman. I could tell by the soot on his face and the red bandanna around his neck. "You looking for fishing worms?" He laughed.

"No, sir," I said. "We are finding coal that falls from the cars."

"It's mighty dangerous for two youngsters to be running these tracks," he said. "You tell your daddy he ought to buy coal from now on."

"Our daddy is on sick leave," I informed him. "We ain't got any money to buy food, much less coal."

The fireman stepped away from the window. Buddy and I resumed our search for coal. A second later the man came back to the window. "Hey!" he said. "You little fellows bring that coal bucket over here. I got something for you."

We brought him our bucket. The fireman filled it with good, clean coal straight from the train's own supply.

"What's your name?" I asked the fireman. "I need it to remember you in my prayers tonight."

He smiled the kindest smile I'd seen since coming to Knoxville. He wiped the back of his neck with his red bandanna. "You just call me Jim," he said. "The Lord will know who you're talking about. Now you boys stay away from the train when it comes through day after tomorrow. I'll throw off a scoop of coal for you so you don't have to step on the tracks."

Our bucket was so full of coal it took both of us to carry it home, side by side.

"We might actually be warm tonight!" I said.

Everyone was sure surprised when we bumped our way up to our house with our bucket so full.

"No cinders or clinkers at all," Mama exclaimed, picking out a couple of lumps for the fireplace. "Where did you get all this coal?"

"Our guardian angel gave it to us," I answered. I gave Buddy a wink. "And the day after tomorrow, if we're lucky, we might see him again."

Mama looked at Buddy and me over her glasses. "Does this angel have a name by any chance?"

"Just Jim," I said. "He's guardian angel for us and for the steam engine that pulls the coal cars."

Mama shook her head and went back to fixing supper. The kitchen was already getting warmer.

Two days later, as promised, Buddy and I stood back from the train as it steamed up to the crossing. Jim appeared in the window and gave us a wave. A second later a large scoop of coal flew out of the engine cab, followed by a bright red scrap of cloth.

"Looks like Jim lost his neck bandanna," I said, running over to pick it up. "Wait, there's something tied up in it." I untied the scrap of cloth and pulled it open.

"Well, just look at that," Buddy said. "Two pieces of bubble gum!"

"And a dollar bill!" I said, waving the money in the air. "Our guardian angel must be rich!"

Buddy and I returned to the train tracks regularly all that winter. Three days a week, we met Jim in his engine cab. Each time we received a bucket of coal, and sometimes a treat, like penny candy or money. You can bet I never forgot to put Jim in my prayers each night.

In the spring our family moved back to the mountains. I had never been so happy to see our old house and our gardens, the woods and the streams. City life was not for me. But whenever I thought about Knoxville I smiled, remembering Jim, our guardian angel. I still remember him in my prayers. I still don't know his full name, but the Lord knows exactly who I'm talking about, even all these years later.

Whiteout!

Dolores Wyckoff

DARKNESS PRESSED IN AT MY window. I peered into it, searching for a glimmer of headlights from my husband's four-wheeler. *Where are you, Josh*? I'd been asking for the last hour and a half. It wasn't like him not to be home for dinner by 5:00 PM. Certainly never this late. Winter nights came early here in Anderson, Alaska. It was early evening, but it might as well have been midnight.

I'd tried not to worry. But it was late November, the temperature well below zero and falling fast. Josh had been out since morning at the river, collecting driftwood to add to our woodpile for the long winter months ahead. Worried? I was a nervous wreck!

I tossed on my parka and ran out to the truck. Josh was out there somewhere alone, unprotected, maybe hurt. It was early enough in the season that parts of the river could still not be frozen solid. Josh could fall through false ice and never get out. I had to find him. And quick.

I drove down to the trailhead. No Josh. Out in the dark, the wind whipped through the trees. Usually I loved our home in the wilds of Alaska, surrounded by nature. Only a few hundred people lived in our village. We were independent types. But now the wilderness I loved seemed terrifying. I called Josh's name. Even if he could hear me, he wouldn't be able to trace my voice to the car. The icy wind scattered voices the way it scattered snowflakes.

I backed the truck down the trail. I'd only gone a few feet when the truck stopped moving. I stepped on the gas, but the tires spun in place. That howling wind had polished the frozen road into glass. I was stuck.

Now what? In my worry about Josh, I'd left the house without water. Or a flashlight. No glove warmers. Nothing. Not even an energy bar. I felt completely alone. And however bad I felt, Josh must have been feeling worse. *Dear God, please be with Josh. Send Your angels to protect him.* Were there even such things as arctic angels? Somehow I couldn't picture them bundled up in parkas.

I turned off the engine and stepped out of the truck. I couldn't stand out here for long. I thought of a friend, Linda, from church. She lived a half mile away. I started running, my lungs burning from the cold. The wind picked up. That meant a storm was coming in. I crashed against Linda's front door, my legs barely able to carry me one more step.

She opened the door, her eyes wide. "Dolores?" she said. "What are you doing here?"

"It's Josh," I said, gasping. "He went out this morning and hasn't come back."

"Come in here where it's warm," she said. "I'll call up the fire chief."

I collapsed by her woodstove while she made the call. "He's sending out a search party," she whispered to me as they talked. "He says not to worry."

How could I not worry? I'd struggled to make the walk to Linda's house in this cold. Josh was out there all alone. How long would it take to organize a volunteer rescue team? How many people would even be available? The windows rattled. The storm was getting closer. Soon it would be too dangerous for anyone to be out. Someone definitely needed to worry.

Linda drove me back to my house. I was so grateful not to be alone. I was also grateful for being able to borrow a police scanner from a neighbor. That would allow me to follow the search as it happened. I set up the scanner while Linda called Connie, another friend from church. There was a knock on the door. The fire chief's wife, Wava.

"There's at least twenty men searching and more on the way," she said. "There's men coming in from upriver, from way out in the bush. They're out in twos on snowmobiles."

I poured tea for the three of us. Soon Connie arrived. "I brought an UNO deck," Connie announced, shaking snow out of her hair.

Cards? How could anyone think of playing a game at a time like this? But Connie insisted. While she shuffled the cards I turned up the police scanner to listen to the radio traffic. Voices came and went over the speakers, men checking in with each other out in the woods. It was soothing to listen to them.

But would the help get there in time? Outside the snow was coming down hard. The wind would erase any tracks.

The phone rang, distracting me from my worries. It was my neighbor from across town, just calling to check in. I'd just put down the phone when it instantly rang again and kept ringing. Friends called. Neighbors. People from church. My minister. The Catholic priest. Wives of men Josh worked with at the power plant. People I barely knew. Everyone said the same thing: "We're praying for you and Josh. Let us know if there's anything you need." The ladies in my kitchen were praying, too, when they weren't trying to divert me with a new card game.

Just before midnight a voice crackled over the scanner: "I see the four-wheeler! It's in the river." The room went silent. The man reported the ATV had fallen through a layer of false ice. But there was no sign of Josh.

It seemed forever before anyone spoke. I thought of Josh, freezing, his clothes soaked from the river. Only a matter of time before hypothermia set in. *If it hasn't already.*

"I know it sounds bad," Linda finally said. "But God's still in charge. And those guys aren't going to stop looking until they find him—safe and sound."

She picked up the cards and dealt them. "I don't think you've ever told me what brought you and Josh to Alaska," she said.

"It was just after we married," I said. "Josh's parents lived up here and his dad said he could get him a job. That was twenty-seven years ago. Alaska seemed like the other side of the world…" My voice trailed off.

But my friends were suddenly determined to talk about everything but the search: what they were planning for Thanksgiving, their favorite TV shows, the time Wava fell headfirst into a store freezer trying to get a turkey. I couldn't help but get drawn into their stories. Once or twice I even caught myself laughing. It was 4:00 AM before I realized it. Nearly eighteen hours since Josh had left the house. But I couldn't be distracted forever. "What if—" I began.

The scanner crackled. Someone spoke. "I hear him." Linda squeezed my hand. Everyone listened now.

Ten minutes passed with no further reports. I could hear the men calling Josh's name. The sound was urgent, haunting—like a life-and-death game of blind man's bluff in the wind.

"No sign of him here!"

"Don't move, Josh! Let us come to you!"

I leaned forward, perched on the edge of my seat. *If there are angels in Alaska, we need them now.*

The sun was just peeking over the horizon when the cry came over the scanner: "I've got him!"

We rushed to the trailhead. Four men carried Josh out of the woods on a stretcher. His eyes were barely open. But to me he'd never looked better.

Hours later, at the hospital, Josh told me his four-wheeler had fallen through the ice. He'd made it to shore, but with his clothes wet his only hope was to keep moving to generate body heat. The snow and wind were blinding. He couldn't find his way home.

"But then I heard the voices of the rescuers," Josh said. "They were all around me. I couldn't see them, but I knew they would find me. That sound kept me alive. They sounded like...just like angels."

I thought again of that sound of the men faithfully calling into the night, never a thought of turning back. God *had* sent angels. By the dozens. Angels calling on the phone, playing UNO, telling funny stories. They'd come wearing parkas and driving snowmobiles. Rugged, caring, beautiful, cold weather–loving angels especially made for Alaska.

Stalled on the Tracks

Luis Vega

THAT MORNING, EVEN BEFORE MY wife, Rossana, and I left the house with our five-year-old son, Alex, I had a kind of premonition. It was as if I sensed that God had special plans for me that day. Usually Rossana drove me to Caprio's Restaurant in nearby Delray Beach, where I worked as a chef. On this particular morning, however, something told me to get behind the wheel.

We hadn't been on our way long when we reached the railroad tracks in Boca Raton. High-speed passenger trains roar through here every day. As we approached the gates, the red light began flashing and a warning clanged, so I stopped. The driver of the car in the lane to the left of me accelerated as if she were going to hurry across before the gates came down. But then, probably thinking better of it, she suddenly braked to a halt. The woman behind her couldn't stop in time and banged into the car, shoving it onto the tracks.

The crossing gates came down, leaving the stalled automobile straddling the rails. The oncoming train's warning horn pierced our ears as it roared closer.

The woman was alone in the car. She just sat there.

"Why doesn't she get out?" I cried. Other drivers were honking and screaming.

My blood ran cold at what was about to happen. I do not consider myself a courageous person, but something came over me as I sat trembling. A powerful force energized me. I slid from behind the wheel and raced to the tracks where the woman sat in the auto with her head down.

"Get out of the car!" I yelled. She seemed paralyzed with fear.

The train's horn deafened me, and the ground shook under my feet.

"Get out!" I screamed as she looked up at me with a blank stare. In panic I glanced back at my wife. Her face was white as she called for me to get away. For an instant I wanted to run back to safety—but I couldn't.

What happened next passed in a terrifying blur. As the monstrous red-white-and-blue-striped nose of the engine with its blazing-white light rushed toward us, I wrested the car door open, yanked the woman out, and leaped aside with her as the locomotive hurtled into the car. The earsplitting explosion sent shock waves through me as the train, its wheels blazing sparks, bulldozed the crumpled car far down the tracks.

Later, when the woman was able to speak, she hugged me, calling me her guardian angel. "God sent you to save me," she said, weeping. I am certainly not an angel, but I do believe God sent me. I couldn't have done what I did by myself. For as we are told in Isaiah 40:29 (KJV), God "giveth power to the faint; and to them that have no might he increaseth strength."

One Last Hug

Jeneane Denger

"Another year, another Home and Garden show," I said. My husband, Charlie, sold and installed patio enclosures, so each year we sat in one of his models while people checked out his merchandise. Sometimes it meant a lot of sitting and waiting for customers to show real interest, and that gave us time to talk. Our conversation lately had centered on one sad topic—our young granddaughter, Rachel, who had died less than a year ago.

Her bright smile, her laughter, and best of all, the hugs she used to give—Charlie and I would never tire of recalling every tiny detail about the child we loved so much and lost so early. We had our memories if we couldn't have that little precious life itself. *Oh, but what I wouldn't give for one last hug from Rachel*, I thought.

A family with three little boys stopped by our booth. The youngest looked like he might have been about three, just like Rachel. Charlie and I watched him pal around with his brothers. Then, in the blink of an eye, the little rascal pulled the sliding-glass door of the patio model shut with all his might—and locked us in!

The boy's father quickly took the boy's hand and reopened the door to rescue us. "Sorry, folks!" he said. Just as the family was walking away, the boy turned and ran toward me. He opened his arms wide as I bent down. He gave me a long, tender hug, just like the kind I used to get from Rachel. Then he ran back to his parents, and they were gone.

God hears every prayer, no matter how big or small. Getting a hug from a child seems like a small thing under the circumstances, but God knew it was a big deal to me.

The Englishman

Joan Wester Anderson

LISA GALLAGHER'S FATHER WAS A diplomat, so she had logged many travel miles. When she was ten, her father announced that the family would be moving to Africa, stopping in Paris for a few days of sightseeing. Lisa was thrilled—Paris was such a beautiful place! But one evening as the family strolled the Champs-Élysées, Lisa got ahead of her family. "I turned around and they were nowhere in sight!" Lisa says. "I panicked and stumbled down a side street." A very proper Parisian doorman saw her distress, "but he couldn't understand a word I said," Lisa explained. "He went inside the restaurant to grab the first English speaker he could find."

Out came a very dignified Englishman, who calmly listened to Lisa's predicament. "Come," he said, grabbing his coat. "Let's see what we can do."

"But your dinner…" Lisa realized that the gentleman was leaving his companions to help her, and she was embarrassed.

"Not to worry," he reassured her as he hailed a cab. Within minutes they had arrived at his hotel, where he ordered a plate of snacks for Lisa, then asked the hotel phone operators to call the American Embassy. Lisa had forgotten the name of their family's hotel, but she did know where her father worked. Soon they would connect.

"While we were waiting, my dad and brother were running up and down the Champs-Élysées in the dark, frantically searching every business and side street," Lisa recalls. "My mother stayed at the hotel so someone would be there in case of a call (no cell phones then). The operators did eventually reach someone at the Embassy who knew my dad and knew where we were staying so they were able to call our hotel and talk to my mother to let her know where I was."

Eventually Lisa's father checked with the hotel and discovered where Lisa was. He ran all the way to her location. Lisa was never so glad to see anyone in her life! Father and daughter both thanked the kind gentleman profusely. He brushed away their gratitude. "I was glad to help," he told them. "I have a daughter close to Lisa's age, and if she were lost, I hope someone would do the same for her." Off he went to return to his dinner party while Lisa and her father walked back to their hotel. "I think I believe in guardian angels now," Lisa's father said, only half in jest. But that was not the end of the story.

A few months later, after the family settled in Dar es Salaam, Tanzania, on the east coast of Africa, Lisa signed up to take horseback riding lessons at the tiny Sunny Horse Ranch. During the first lesson, there was only one other rider, a girl about Lisa's age. The beginner ring was very small and the girls were led around it by a *sise* (ranch hand), and because of the slow pace, the girls chatted a lot. "As we were talking I looked over the hedge and saw a tall Englishman standing and watching us," Lisa says. She stared for a moment. It couldn't be—but the tall man was her rescuer from Paris!

"That man!" she said to her riding companion. "I know him!"

The other girl smiled. "I know him too," she told Lisa. "He's my father!"

Lisa was stunned. "My parents are divorced," the other girl went on. "My mother and I live in Tanzania, and my father lives in England, but he's here right now to visit me."

Lisa was still speechless. When the class ended, she jumped off her horse and ran over to the gentleman. "Do you remember me?" she asked him. "From Paris?"

The Englishman was as surprised as Lisa. "I just remember him stroking his moustache and saying over and over, 'How *extroooooooordnry*,' just like that," Lisa says. "What would the odds be of a little American girl getting lost in Paris and found by an Englishman and then running into him several months later at a tiny little horse ranch in Africa?"

In all the amazement, no one thought to exchange addresses. "So I let my guardian angel slip away," Lisa says today. "I truly believe he was that. My only wish is that I had some way to look him up and thank him."

Angels are beautiful spirits. And sometimes a real person can show us all how to be more like them.

The Angel in the Red Jacket

Susan Elizabeth Hale

"CAN YOU HELP ME? I need to find the platform for Aberystwyth," I nervously asked the attendant in England's noisy Birmingham New Street Station.

The man muttered something in a thick English accent, pointing down the track. Brakes screeched. People shuffled past.

"I'm sorry, I didn't understand. Which way is the platform for Wales?"

He spoke louder, his voice an irritated drone. I still didn't understand. "I need help." We looked at each other. "I need help!" I said, bursting into tears.

It had been a long travel day. Aching from clunking my luggage up and down stairs, my arms were shaky. My first train was late, making me miss my booked ticket to the next one. Would I even make my train to Wales now? Traveling alone from America, I was on my way to teach at a voice conference. Adding to my upset, I had no way to reach the person picking me up at the station in Aberystwyth.

"Wait right here." The man left. Within minutes a customer service attendant appeared, a young man in a red jacket. His name tag read "Vinnie."

"Are you all right, madame? Come with me. I'll get you sorted," he said, wheeling my luggage through the maze of tracks to a lift. "Where are you going?"

"Wolverhampton on my way to Aberystwyth."

"You've already missed the Wolverhampton train. There be another in an hour."

Once above in the crowded station, he reached into his pocket, pulling out a silver twenty pence coin. "In case you need to use the Ladies." I did. When I returned, a hot cup of tea and a table at a café were waiting for me. "Stay here, madame. I'll come back when I have more information."

Ten minutes later he arrived to tell me I would need to take two more trains. I'd arrive in Aberystwyth after midnight, making me at least four hours late. "Don't worry. I've arranged for help with your bags along the way. Just look for the people with red jackets when you get off. I'll be back to get you on the train to Wolverhampton."

Tea, Vinnie's kindness and care calmed my nerves and comforted me to continue onward into my now late-night journey.

Vinnie returned with an assistant, an East Indian man. They both escorted me to the platform to wait. I offered him a tip. "I couldn't accept that, madame. This is my job. It's been my pleasure." Reaching into my pocket, I found a small white turtle, carved from a Zuni bead from the Southwest. It was my touchstone to home and I'd been carrying it with me. "Would you accept this?"

"Oh, Vinnie—" the other man said, nodding. "Turtles are most auspicious. You should take the turtle." Smiling, Vinnie took the small gift and helped me on the train with my luggage.

I made all my connections easily with my new red-jacket helpers. There was even someone waiting to meet me at Aberystwyth who took me to my dorm room at the college where the conference was to be held.

Checking into my room, I noticed a note waiting for me. "Your husband called." *I'll call tomorrow,* I thought. Exhausted, I fell asleep. The next morning another note appeared under my door. "Call your brother," it read. Who's died? My mother or my father? They both shared a room in the same nursing home in California. I left knowing they were in good hands while I was out of the country. I searched my heart. I knew my father was dead. The last time I saw him Alzheimer's had taken his mind. He spoke only in broken sentences, lists of incoherent words. But as he looked over at the love of his life asleep in bed, he said, "Isn't she beautiful?" Then looking into my eyes, said, "Gee, I love you, Susie." Alzheimer's had not taken his heart. These were the last words I heard my father say.

Phone calls confirmed that he had died. *When?* I wondered. Calculating the time difference, I discovered that he had died when I was at the train station, where I burst into tears asking for help, when a stranger in a red jacket had arrived as my guide.

The conference director was compassionate. She held me and said, "Return home. We understand." I took leave that day. I had to return through Birmingham with only five minutes to make my next connection. When I stepped off the platform, Vinnie was there in his red jacket. "Vinnie!"

"Madame!"

"I only have five minutes to catch the train to Gloucester!"

"Come with me!" He took my bags. We flew through the station. I told him that my father had died the same moment he had helped me before. "Thank you for being there for me, Vinnie." A peacefulness filled me as he ushered me onto the train and we waved good-bye.

Seven years later, traveling again alone in England, I'm back at Birmingham New Street. It feels like yesterday that I was here and my dad was dying. This time I am relaxed and assured.

I see a young man in a red jacket. "Excuse me, is there a man named Vinnie who works here?"

"Yes," he smiled. "He works in the ticket office now. He's over there."

I stood in line. When I got to the window, there he was, a little older, but the same warm brown eyes. "You probably don't remember me. You helped me many years ago."

"I'm sorry but I don't," he said, perplexed. "I help so many people. I can't remember them all."

"Do you remember a woman whose father had just died? I gave you a white turtle."

His face brightened. "Yes, I remember! I have a son now. I gave it to him and he keeps it on the windowsill by his bed."

"Thank you again, Vinnie. My father was a kind man. I know he sent an angel to watch over me. Thank you for being that angel."

An Angel Named Beth

Joan E. McClure

ONE DAY MY FRIEND BOB, who has multiple sclerosis, mentioned how Angus had helped him retrieve something he couldn't reach from his wheelchair. I knew his wife, Rita, and his cat, Patches, but Angus? "Oh, Angus is what I've named my guardian angel," he explained. I'd always been a skeptic but Bob was a pretty smart guy, so I decided maybe there was something to this guardian angel business after all. Still, even if I did have my own angel, the idea of naming it seemed presumptuous.

About a week later I was putting pans away after baking a batch of cookies when I strained my back trying to close the drawer under the oven. I called my handyman to come fix it, but there was no answer. Then the thought of Bob and Angus popped into my head. "God, if I have one," I prayed, "let my guardian angel help me with this drawer."

I heard a knock at the garage door. I couldn't imagine who would come to the garage door at the back of the house, or how anyone had gotten by our dog without him barking. I cautiously opened the door to two older gentlemen in overalls.

"We got your call," one said, "and we've come to fix your door."

"I don't need my door fixed; I need my drawer fixed," I said. "Are you sure you're at the right house? I didn't call you."

He showed me the work order. I admitted that everything except the first name was correct. "This says Beth called," I pointed out. "I'm Joan." I didn't know any Beths.

"But since you're here, could you look at my drawer?" I pleaded. They agreed, and in no time they had it refitted. I tried to pay them, but they refused. "At least take some cookies," I insisted, and off they went, each with a handful of chocolate chip cookies, grinning like schoolboys.

Later that evening, I realized God hadn't just sent me help, He'd actually told me my angel's name.

To Jack in Heaven

Rebecca Baker

NO MATTER HOW GENTLY OUR veterinarian broke the news to me, nothing could prepare me for the shock I felt at having to put our beloved golden retriever, Jack, to sleep. When I walked out of his office, empty blue leash dangling from my hand, I couldn't believe he was gone.

Beside me, my eight-year-old, Daniel, wiped the tears from his own face. He'd bravely insisted on being with his buddy at the end. I was grateful his baby brother, Colin, was too young to understand what was going on.

My husband, Ted, Daniel, and I walked back to the car, where a family friend waited with four-year-old Anna. "Let's go home," Ted said quietly. He started up the car.

"But we forgot Jack," Anna said. "Isn't he coming home with us?"

Ted and I looked sadly at each other. We thought we'd explained all this to Anna. It looked like she hadn't understood after all. "Jack isn't coming home with us, honey," Ted said. "Remember? The vet said he was very sick."

"The vet couldn't make Jack better, Anna," Daniel said.

"Do you understand, sweetie?" I said. "Jack died."

Anna nodded slowly. Ted backed out the car. Then, from the car seat, came Anna's voice again. "But where is he?" she said, starting to cry. "When is he coming home?" Daniel tried to comfort his sister. I looked helplessly at Ted. Her older brother could comprehend what was happening. Her baby brother wasn't aware of anything at all. Poor Anna was stuck in the middle.

That night, when I tucked her into bed, I tried to cheer her up with happy stories of Jack. "When we brought you home from the hospital right after you were born, Jack came running to the door wagging his tail. He couldn't wait to meet you!"

Anna looked longingly at the door to her bedroom. Usually when I tucked Anna into bed Jack would come padding in right behind me. Anna never went to sleep without getting a big, sloppy good-night kiss from Jack. "He's never coming home?" she said. "Ever?"

"Jack was very old," I said. "He didn't feel well. Now he's not sick anymore. He's in heaven with God and the angels. And he's very happy there. I promise."

Was any of this making sense to her? We'd talked about heaven, but this was Anna's first experience with death. She hadn't known anyone else who'd died and gone to heaven. She knew she had family who lived far away. We didn't see them in person, but they loved Anna and knew she loved them in return. That gave me an idea. "Why don't we write a letter to Jack tomorrow?" I said. "You can tell him how much you love him."

Anna smiled. She loved writing letters. I knew she couldn't expect a return letter like she got when she wrote to her aunts and uncles, but maybe just talking to Jack would be a comfort.

Early next morning Anna got out her crayons and we sat down together at the dining room table. Anna selected just the right shade of yellow and drew a circle for a head, followed by a circle body and four circle legs. Then she added Jack's long, feathery tail. "Jack loved to play house," she said as she drew. "And dress up."

"He could never keep those sunglasses on, could he?" I said, remembering good old Jack sitting patiently in his dress while Anna arranged jewelry around his neck.

Anna selected another crayon to make a stick figure with long hair next to Jack. Then she added a bright yellow sun. When the portrait was finished she dictated a letter. "Jack is sick. So now he is in heaven," she said. "I love you and miss you." She signed her name herself in lopsided letters. "Now we need to send this to Jack."

I placed the letter in an envelope and wrote the address in block letters: TO JACK IN HEAVEN. Anna licked the envelope and together we put it in the mailbox. Our mail carrier looked a little confused when she picked the letter up a couple of hours later. But I went outside to quickly explain the situation. "No problem," she said, and slipped the letter in her bag.

Once the letter was gone, I could only hope I'd done the right thing. Anna's questions seemed to have stopped, but I wondered if she could really understand that Jack was in a truly happy place. And because of that, we could be happy for him. "She'll understand it in her own time," said Ted one day after yet another discussion.

Just before lunch, there was a knock on the door. It was someone from the post office. He held up a box wrapped in brown paper. "Are you Miss Anna Baker?" he asked, looking down.

Anna nodded shyly.

"I have a special delivery for you."

The box was addressed to Anna. The return address read: JACK IN HEAVEN. Anna ran with her box to the kitchen. "I manage the post office and saw your letter," the man explained. "We lost our family dog recently. I have a daughter too."

Back in the kitchen with Anna, I helped her unwrap the package. She pulled out a book about a puppy and a stuffed dog that looked a lot like Jack. She squeezed the dog to her chest. "There's a letter too!" she said. "Read it, Mommy!"

"Dear Anna," I read. "I have arrived safely in heaven."

Anna's eyes got wide. "Does he like it there?"

I continued. "It is really nice here. The other dogs and I play ball and swim all day. There are many squirrels to chase here and all the mail carriers have bones in their bags for us."

Anna giggled.

"My bed here isn't as comfy as yours, but I want you to know that God takes good care of me here." I looked down at Anna, who nodded slowly. *She understands that,* I thought. Jack went on to say how happy he was to receive Anna's letter. "I miss my family. I miss you," he finished up. "God sends His blessings and wants you to know that He loves you. We will both be watching over you. Love, Jack." I folded up the letter and handed it to Anna. She danced around the kitchen.

That night I tucked Anna into bed with her new stuffed dog beside her. "Jack is in heaven," she said. "Jack is happy there. And that makes me happy too."

Anna would be fine, I knew. Thanks to a letter that truly did come from heaven. By way of a post office angel with a loving heart.

Angel on the Bridge

Delores Topliff

As red warning lights flashed and loud sirens blared, my eleven-year-old legs pumped back and forth along the pedestrian walk from one part of the Interstate Bridge center spans to the other. The large white barricade had dropped down on that long bridge crossing the Columbia River between Oregon and Washington. But which portion would go up? The center part rises more than one hundred feet for large ships and barges to pass beneath. Terrified, I ran back and forth, desperate to know which part of the barricade was safe to be on to avoid the vertical lift. The only problem was, I couldn't tell which part would rise. And there was no more time left for guesswork.

Mowing lawns at one dollar a yard with a push mower helped me save money to buy surprise Christmas presents for my family. I couldn't wait and begged permission from Mom to ride the Greyhound bus alone for my first time from Vancouver, Washington, to Portland, Oregon. Nearby, the Farmer's Market near the depot offered great handmade gifts and inexpensive snacks. I carefully checked and boarded the right bus to return home. Peering through the window I watched scenery slide by, searching for the right place to get off. After passing North Portland's Speedway Race Track and the Jantzen Beach Amusement Park, I knew I was close. I pulled the buzzer and got off.

Even before hitting the bottom step, I knew I was getting off too soon. I should have stayed on but was too embarrassed to say so. I was on the Oregon side of the river, when I should have crossed the bridge to Vancouver. But I had good legs. And determination. I'd cross the bridge—and walk six more miles to our subdivision.

Mom was home with my baby sister. Cell phones weren't invented. I plodded onto the bridge. Except I hadn't known an ocean-going vessel might pass underneath at this exact moment, making sirens screech, lights flash, and the heavy barricade swing down in front of me, meaning the center portion was about to rise. Desperately rushing back and forth, eyes huge, I didn't know which part of the bridge was safe. Where could I go to avoid being taken up? All four lines of traffic had stopped, two from the north, and two from the south. If I ended up on the vertical lift, I might die.

Just then I heard the long blast of a pickup truck horn. And then heard it again. The dark blue company truck one lane over and two vehicles back that read City of Vancouver Water Department on its door. The driver opened his passenger door and waved me over. My grandfather! Mom's dad. Vancouver's water inspector who tested drinking water in our water towers, and let me accompany him sometimes. I'd never been so glad to see him in my life. He looked disbelieving, but happy too. Exhaling a huge sigh of relief, I ran over and climbed in.

"What are you doing here?" His frown now made his dark eyebrows meet.

"Went to Portland, got off the bus too soon."

"What on earth is your mother thinking, letting you go alone?"

"I begged her. Told her I was old enough. Earned money for Christmas presents and was excited to buy them." I collapsed against his passenger seat.

The bridge portion one vehicle ahead of us, just past the barricade, slowly rose and lowered again as we watched the massive ship pass below. Grandpa shook his head. "I don't understand. My job never takes me to Portland, except it did today. I can't believe I was here now. Just when you needed me." He shook his head again. "It's crazy. You were frantic."

"Yes," I answered softly, clutching the armrest so I wouldn't cry. "I couldn't tell which side was safe."

"I'll take you home. And talk to your mother."

"Thanks," I squeaked.

Six miles was farther than I thought. Grandpa made it clear he was unhappy. After his talk with Mom, my tail feathers got clipped. He explained that bridge openings last ten minutes and happen only ten to twenty times a month. "Thank God He had me there then." He shook his head again.

I shivered every time I thought of it, and still never cross that bridge without remembering. It was two more years before I was allowed to try solo trips again.

My favorite Bible verse became the one in Matthew about God seeing every sparrow—that not a single one falls outside of His care.

I'm thankful that on that frightening day on the Interstate Bridge, He saw an adventurous eleven-year-old, and rescued her before she fell.

Runaway Car!

Marilyn Morgan King

MY HUSBAND WAS OUT OF town on business, and the spring day was too inviting to waste on loneliness; so with my two children, their playmate from across the street, and a picnic lunch, I drove to the lake a few miles from town.

The children remembered the last time we had been to the lake we had brought sleds and skates, so they were excited to see green trees and blue water where spidery branches and gray-white snow had been.

"God has used the magic of the warm sun and spring rains to wake up the trees and flowers," I told them.

"You mean," said five-year-old Karen, "God has been here before us and done all that?"

"Yes, and He's still here. God is everywhere."

"Why does He wake them up?"

That was a tough one. "Well, I guess because He loves all living things and wants to take good care of them," I answered, choosing my words carefully. Before she could pose another question, a frightened squirrel darted across an opening. She watched wide-eyed.

As we explored the lake, we made a game of looking for evidence of God. The children picked some wildflowers and put them on the picnic table in a paper cup filled with lake water, and we thanked God for them before we ate our lunch.

When we were ready to leave, Karen and her friend, Susan, wanted to go to the restroom, so I parked the car on the knoll by the bathrooms. Paul, my two-year-old, and I waited for them in the car.

When Susan came back to tell me that Karen needed help with her sunsuit, I pulled on the emergency brake, told Paul to wait in the car, and went up the hill.

I had just stepped inside when I heard Susan scream. I rushed out to see the car rolling backward, off the road, and down the slope toward the high embankment—which marked a steep drop-off into the lake. The emergency brake had failed!

Something seemed to explode inside my chest as I ran, shrieking, after the runaway car. But there was nothing I could do! It was moving too fast—farther and farther away from me. In a rush of panic, I realized that there was no hope. Paul was on his way over that cliff to certain death.

Yet, incredulously, I heard myself saying, "Thank God." Thank God? How I could be saying that in such a moment is beyond me. However, in that instant when there was no logical hope I knew—yes, knew—that Paul would be saved.

It was almost simultaneous with that thought that a young boy came out of nowhere. He ran alongside the moving car, fighting desperately to pull the door open and get inside. The cliff loomed closer. Another thought crowded into my mind: They would both be killed!

Then the youngster disappeared inside the car. It swerved to the right, still heading toward the embankment sideways. But as the right side of the car came to the brink, it slowed and seesawed on the ledge, seemingly hanging by its left wheels. As though defying gravity, it balanced precariously on the edge.

It is still going over, I thought. Then I began running again.

As I ran, I saw the boy scoop Paul in his arms, jump out, and carry him to safety. When I reached Paul and the boy, I hugged them both, crying in near hysteria. The car teetered for a moment, then steadied on the ledge.

After a few minutes, I got control of myself and tried as best I could to find words to express my joy. The boy's name was Robert Royle, and I remember telling him that I knew positively God had sent him. He shrugged his part off with this explanation:

"My folks decided to walk around the lake and I started to go with them but changed my mind. There's a good view of the boats from here."

It was a simple, logical answer, one that could be accepted at face value and forgotten. I, however, choose to believe that God did take part in this one small episode in life, just as I believe He is interested in all His creations. I thought back to the question Karen had posed earlier in the day about the spring awakening of trees and flowers.

"Why does He wake them up?" she had asked.

"Because He loves all living things and wants to take good care of them," I had told her.

The depth of that love and the tenderness of that care were revealed to me on a bright spring day.

CHAPTER 3

Angels Watching over Me

Angel Medallion

Ingrid Shelton

DECEMBER IS ESPECIALLY HARD FOR me since my husband, Philip, died. One afternoon, about three weeks before Christmas, I was at my dresser thinking about Philip when my eyes fell on a small silver medallion with an angel on it.

Where did that come from? I thought. I live alone, and no one had been in my bedroom. I turned the medallion over. Three words were engraved on the back: *Always With You.*

Now, I keep the medallion on a table near my front door. My husband may be in heaven, but he's still with me—and so are God's angels—all year round.

My Cart Runneth Over

Gail Tucker

NORMALLY, I'M THE FIRST ONE to be in the Thanksgiving spirit, but as I pushed my cart through the grocery store I wished we could skip it this year. I passed the turkey, stuffing, and pumpkin pie without a glance. Mom wouldn't be with us, and neither would anyone else. What kind of Thanksgiving was that?

Mom was in the hospital and not doing well. Our two sons were living out of state and wouldn't be able to make the long drive. Friends had invited us over, but I wasn't feeling up to it. "I'm just not very good company right now," I'd told them. Distraught was more like it, with not much to feel thankful for.

I tossed a head of lettuce into my cart to go with the roast I had at home. Turkey and fixings could wait till next year. With just Dale and me to cook for, why make a feast?

I wheeled my cart into the checkout line. The woman bagging groceries chatted with the couple in front of me. "Y'all havin' guests?" She sounded genuinely interested. Friendly and warm. For a minute, she almost made me forget about my troubles.

"Hi there!" she said, smiling when it was my turn. "You plannin' on cookin' at home today?"

"Yes…yes, I am," I said.

"*Hmm*…say, do you like turkey?"

"Love it," I answered.

"How 'bout cranberry salad?"

"Yes, that too."

"And pumpkin pie?"

I nodded. "My favorite." She was describing one of my usual Thanksgiving spreads to a T. *But I won't be having any of that this year,* I thought.

"Well, how would you like to have all of those things and more, already cooked—ready for you to eat and enjoy? And it's on the house!"

Huh? "Why me?" I asked.

"Just come this way," she said, avoiding my question entirely. Together we walked over to the manager's office. "I've got a taker!" she shouted. Into my cart went two large boxes brimming with food. Dale and I would have a feast after all.

"I didn't mean to make you cry," she said.

The words tumbled out before I could stop them. I told her all about Mom. How Dale and I would be eating alone and that I just wasn't up to cooking a traditional Thanksgiving dinner. And worst of all, how I'd lost sight of the fact that we can always find *something* to be thankful for, even in tough times.

"Aw, c'mon now," she said, wrapping me in a big hug. "Obviously, you needed this gift today. And I'll be sure to say some prayers for your mama."

By the time I got back home, I was so excited about our dinner that I practically ran through the front door. "Dale! Dale! You won't believe what I've got!"

I told him all about the woman bagging groceries at the supermarket. We fixed ourselves a couple of plates. I said the grace before we dug in: "Lord, thank You for this food and for the kindness of strangers."

A few weeks later, I drove to the same supermarket to tell the woman what a delicious Thanksgiving we'd had. She wasn't there. I tried describing her to the manager, but he didn't seem to know who I was talking about. In fact, I've shopped there nearly every week since, and I've yet to see her again. I like to think of her as my supermarket angel. She filled more than my cart that Thanksgiving. She filled my heart with thanksgiving.

God Sent His Angels

Joan Wester Anderson

CONNIE KENNEDY OF PAWHUSKA, OKLAHOMA, has the best job in the entire world. Just as I do. We're grandmothers! But there is an enormous amount of responsibility that accompanies this task, and one day Connie's angels were really put to the test.

"I had recently purchased a new car," says Connie, "and I wasn't aware of all its safety features. Along with the car, we had also purchased a top-of-the-line car seat for our eighteen-month-old granddaughter, Jennifer." Eventually Connie felt more confident, and she decided to do some errands on a day when she was caring for Jennifer by herself.

"I was on a highway and Jennifer was in her new car seat, which I thought was correctly strapped down, in the backseat," Connie recalls. The locks on the back doors were also child-proof. But Connie hadn't realized that she had to enable the locks first.... Now the car was on a long expanse of highway where some construction was going on. Connie was leading about fifteen cars along a one-lane stretch when, all of a sudden, the back door next to Jennifer flew open! Shocked, Connie realized that the toddler had managed to undo the car seat and open the lock. Her car seat, barely strapped to the seat, was wobbling around—any minute she could somersault right out of the seat and onto the pavement.

Jennifer hadn't slid anywhere, however. Instead she was waving out the back window. "Hi, hi!" she kept calling while wearing a huge smile. "Her face was lit up like a spotlight," Connie says. "I couldn't see anything out there in the fields for her to be waving at... and although I was in a panic to stop, with the construction trucks all over, there was no place to pull off."

Forcing herself to be calm, Connie talked to Jennifer. "Hold on to your seat, honey," she murmured. "Grandma will stop in just a minute." But Jennifer was absorbed in whatever was outside her window. "She kept laughing, smiling, and even pointing." Finally after about five hundred yards, Connie was able to pull off on a side curb, get out, hug Jennifer, relock everything, and shakily make her way back onto the highway.

Jennifer was completely calm during the whole incident, smiling and extending her little hands to something Connie couldn't see. "But I know what was happening," Connie says. "Jennifer should have plummeted out of the car seat and onto the road, maybe even been run over by the long stream of cars behind us. But something held her inside until I could get us to safety.

"Thank God for guardian angels. I know they were with us that day."

The Snakebite

Debbie Durrance

WE HAD JUST FINISHED SUNDAY dinner when our twelve-year-old son, Mark, asked if he and his dog, Bo, could go out into the field beyond our house for a while. "Just be careful," my husband told him. It was the advice Bobby always gave our children whenever they went out alone, especially in the three years since we'd moved thirty miles out into the brushland of southwestern Florida. Several of our animals had been bitten by rattlesnakes.

As I cleared away the dinner dishes, I watched Mark and Bo race off through the orange and lemon trees of our private oasis. Mark had become so self-reliant out here in the country, I thought.

I took my time with the dishes, enjoying the slow Sunday afternoon, and was just finishing up when I heard the living-room door open. Suddenly our older son, Buddy, yelled, "Mark, what's wrong?" I threw down the dish towel and ran toward the living room just as Mark gasped, "I—I've been rattlesnake-bit—" There was a dull thud. When I got there, Mark was on the floor, unconscious. "Go get your dad. Hurry!" I said to Buddy.

I pulled off Mark's shoe; his foot had already swollen into a large, ugly purple mass. There was a musky odor about him, the same odor we'd noticed the times our animals had been bitten by rattlesnakes. In seconds, Bobby rushed in and grabbed Mark up in his arms. "Come on," he said. "We've got to get him to the emergency center."

We ran and climbed into the cab of Bobby's work truck. I held Mark on my lap, Buddy sat in the middle, and Bobby drove. "Oh, God," I prayed, "help us." It was seventeen miles to the emergency center, and every minute counted.

Mark was unconscious, and convulsions jerked his body. I tried to hold him still, with his face close to mine. As long as I could feel his breath against my cheek, I knew he was still alive. But the soft flutters were becoming weaker and less frequent.

"Hurry, Bobby—please hurry!" I pleaded as he frantically passed car after car. Buddy sat in the center, quietly struggling to hold his brother's legs. None of us dared say it, but we all knew we were in a race against death.

As we neared the business section, steam started to seep out from under the hood of the truck. The motor was overheating. About a mile from the clinic, the motor began to pop and sputter.

I glanced over at Bobby. What would we do if the motor stopped? But before I could get the words out, Bobby had to brake for a slower vehicle and the motor cut off completely. I clutched Mark to me, trying to hold on to whatever life was left. We were right in the middle of traffic. Cars were pulling around us and honking their horns. Bobby jumped out and tried to flag down one of the motorists, but the cars just sped around him. "Why won't they stop?" Buddy sighed.

Desperate by now, Bobby ran over and pulled Mark from my arms. He carried him out to the rear of the car, where the other drivers could see him, but still the cars kept going by. Finally one old compact car stopped. The driver appeared to be a Haitian farm worker, and he didn't understand English. But he could tell we needed help.

"Thank you, thank you…, Bobby shouted as he pulled open the door and pushed Buddy in the backseat. Then he laid Mark down beside him and waved the driver off as I jumped in the front.

"We have to get to the emergency center!" I cried, but his questioning look told me he didn't understand. I pointed in the direction we should go.

As we pulled away, I glanced back at Bobby standing in the street. There was no room for him in the small car and our truck was blocking traffic, but I wished he could be with me.

At the emergency center, medical technicians started working on Mark immediately, trying to stabilize his condition. They started fluids and began artificial respiration. But soon after Bobby arrived, the emergency technicians told us they had done all they could and were transferring Mark to Naples Community Hospital, where Dr. Michael Nycum would meet us.

By the time we arrived at the hospital, Mark had stopped breathing twice and had gone into a coma. For the next twelve hours we waited and prayed while the doctors and nurses worked constantly with him. We could tell by the looks on their faces that they didn't expect him to make it.

"Folks, about the only thing the little fellow has going for him is his heart— and that's under tremendous strain," Dr. Nycum told us.

We watched helplessly during the next twenty-four hours as the venom attacked every part of his body. His eyes swelled so tight that all we could see were the ends of his eyelashes. His leg was so swollen the doctors had to make long slashes along it to relieve the pressure on the blood vessels. And still they were afraid they might have to amputate.

Then, miraculously, Mark passed the crisis point and began to improve a little. He was still in a coma, and certainly not out of danger, but the swelling began to go down.

After that, each day brought improvement. On Thursday, Bobby and I sat there beside Mark's bed. We were drained, exhausted, prayed out. I was sitting in a chair close to him, holding his hand, when I thought I felt a movement. But no, I told myself, it was probably my imagination. Yet a moment later, there it was again, a faint fluttering of the small hand inside mine.

"Bobby," I said, sitting up and reaching across to him. "Bobby! Mark moved—he moved!"

Bobby summoned the nurses and doctor. Mark was coming out of the coma.

"Mom...Mom...," he moaned.

"Yes, honey, we're here." The words caught in my throat.

"Dad..."

"Yes, son..."

His eyes opened now as he looked over at Bobby. "Dad...are you mad at me?"

"What do you mean?" Bobby tried to laugh, but it came out a little ragged. "Of course I'm not mad at you."

"I was afraid you'd be mad at me for being so careless."

Bobby reached over and patted Mark on the head. "We're just thankful you're getting better. But what happened, son? Do you feel like telling us?"

The nurses and Dr. Nycum moved a little closer.

"Well, Bo and I spotted a bird in a cabbage palm and, well, I guess I wasn't paying too much attention to where I was going. I was looking at the bird and jumped over the ditch...and my foot landed on something that moved when I hit it.

"And then it was like something slammed down hard on my foot, and my leg started getting real hot. When I looked down, I saw a big rattler had hold of my shoe—it was biting on my foot. It was hurting so bad and Bo was barking and jumping at the snake, but it wouldn't let go. Then Bo jumped on the snake and tore into its head. It let go and crawled off into the bushes.

"Dad, I tried to remember what you said to do if we ever got snakebit, but I was hurting so bad, and getting weak and dizzy. I was a long way from the house, and I knew none of you would hear me if I called..."

"But where were you, Mark?" Bobby asked.

"Out in the field, a long ways from the house. Out there next to the ditch in the field."

"But that's a third of a mile from the house. How did you get to the house?"

Dr. Nycum shook his head. "Medically speaking, it would have been impossible for him to have walked that far."

Bobby and I looked uncertainly at each other. There were also the thirteen steps up to our front door—he'd had to climb those too. I took a deep breath. After everything that had happened, I was almost afraid to ask, but I had to know, "How did you get back to the house, Mark?"

"Well, I remembered you and Dad saying that the more you moved, the quicker the poison would reach your heart, and I knew I couldn't run. But I was so scared, and all I wanted to do was get home. I probably would have run if I could have, but I couldn't because it hurt so bad. And then...Dad, there's something I have to tell you. About the man."

"The man? What man?" Bobby asked. "Was someone out there with you?"

"Yes—I mean, no—I mean, I don't know. All I know is that he carried me..."

"He carried you?"

"Yes, when I couldn't make it to the house. He picked me up." I could feel a tingle on the back of my neck.

"He talked to me in a real deep voice," Mark went on, "and told me that I was going to be real sick, but that I'd be all right."

"What did he look like?" I asked Mark shakily.

"I couldn't see his face, Mom. All I could see was that he had on a white robe, and his arms were real strong. He reached down and picked me up. And I was hurting so bad, I just sort of leaned my head over on him. He carried me to the house and up the steps. When he put me down, I held on to the door and turned around, and—"

His blue eyes stared into mine with an earnestness I'd never seen before. "All I could see was his back."

For a long time, none of us could speak; it was almost more than we could take in. "God is our refuge and strength," I said to myself, "a very present help in trouble" (Psalm 46:1, RSV).

For most of my life I had believed that passage in the Bible by faith. Now I saw the proof of it.

"Mom...Dad...," Mark said, hesitating. "I know you may not believe me—"

"We believe you," I whispered as Bobby put his arm around me. "We believe you."

The Warm Quilt

Betty Carter

THE HOSPITAL DELIVERY ROOM WAS cold, so cold. Or maybe it was just me. I shivered from head to toe. I hadn't felt that way when delivering my first three children, but everything about this pregnancy was different.

My due date had come and gone, with several bouts of false labor. The doctor finally decided to give me a hormone to speed up the birth process. It seemed like the IV drip the nurse had put in my arm was pumping ice water into my veins.

Jim, my husband, stood by my side in his mask and hospital scrubs, holding my hand. Nurses bustled in and out of the room, checking me often as the labor progressed. I didn't say anything about the cold. I didn't want to worry anybody.

An older nurse I hadn't seen before walked across the room and laid her hand on my right shoulder. "My goodness, you need warming up," she said. "I'll be back."

She returned quickly with a quilt that felt fresh from the dryer. I snuggled into its soft, heavenly warmth. My shivers subsided.

Labor progressed and soon I gave birth to a healthy baby boy, weighing in at six pounds, eleven ounces.

I was taken to another room to rest. Jim sat next to me. "I'm so glad the nurse brought me that warm quilt," I told him. "I was so cold, I didn't think I could make it."

Jim looked at me oddly. "I was right there beside you. Nobody brought in a quilt."

Rainy Day Angel

Kelly Gallagher

"GOING FOR A BIKE RIDE! See you later!" I called to my mother as I bounded through the kitchen to the back door.

"*Mmm*," Mom said from the couch, her fingers tangled in crocheting yarn, eyes fixed on the game show on TV. Dad didn't respond. He was engrossed in his music reference book. Just like every night. *My life is so boring*, I thought, letting the screen door slam behind me.

Everything was always the same. School, homework, bed, repeat. An endless loop through all of my thirteen years. Mom and Dad always did and said the exact same things. So boring. A bike ride was the best I could do for excitement—and how unexciting was that? A light mist fell from the sky as I walked to the shed, determined to get out of the house despite the iffy spring weather, which had been wet and dreary for days. Finally it was clear enough to go for one quick spin.

I hopped on my bike. A lot of kids from school couldn't go anywhere without adult supervision. But here on Willow Lane, no one worried. Nothing dangerous—or exciting—ever happened on our quiet cul-de-sac. Willow Lane was surrounded by fields and woods. There were only nine families on the entire street, and we all knew one another. I'd explored every inch of land.

There was nothing new here for me. No one to meet. Nothing to discover. Nothing surprising.

I rode down Willow Lane, then turned off the road to head up to the orchard next to the street. There was a well-worn path there, steep enough to let me gather decent speed. I reached the crest of the hill and stopped to look at the sunset, but the hues were muted thanks to the oncoming rain. A soft breeze blew back strands of hair that had come loose from my brown ponytail. Rain was on its way again. I put my feet back on the pedals and pushed.

My tires sped over gullies and bumps, splashing through puddles. Behind me, something moved. I turned my head to look. A herd of deer! I glanced at the path and back to the deer again.

I felt a jolt. My front tire had hit something. I jackknifed to the right and flew over the handlebars. The apple trees and the golden grass swirled into scribbles. I landed—hard—and knocked my head. The world went black.

When I came to, the sun had almost set. Waves of pain undulated through my limbs. My head ached. Rocks poked my body. My bike rested on my legs, the upturned wheels still spinning. Light rain began to fall on my face. It took a moment for me to realize where I was, and what had happened. I was just riding my bike, and then...

I have to get home, I thought. I heaved the bike off me. It took all of my energy. I lay back down. Blackness began to creep in again. *Maybe if I just lie here a little while...* The world receded.

I heard a voice. "Are you okay?"

My eyes fluttered open and I lifted my head just high enough to see Willow Lane in the distance. A figure stood on the road. A woman in a bright yellow rain-coat. I squinted my eyes and tried to make out her face, but the oncoming night shadowed her features. She didn't reach for me. She stood still, totally still, as if a part of the landscape. As if she belonged there.

"Are you okay?" she repeated, her voice clear despite the breeze blowing across the orchard. Slowly, I sat up. For a moment, my physical pain was replaced by a feeling of warmth. It was as if the woman had knelt beside me and comforted me. But that was silly. She hadn't so much as moved.

"Yes," I croaked. "I'm okay."

"You get home, then. And take care of yourself," she said. She turned and continued down Willow Lane. I watched her till she disappeared, then dragged myself to my feet. After a few minutes of deep, deliberate breathing, I made my way through the fields, heading back to my house. The yellow lights from my parents' kitchen shone through the window and illuminated the backyard. If I could just get to that familiar light, I'd be okay. Finally my hand grasped the doorknob. I fell into the house.

"Kelly!" my mom said. "What happened?" She bent down to pull me up. "You're bleeding!" Soon we were on our way to the hospital. Fat drops of rain hit the windshield as we drove.

"Who's the president?" the doctor asked when we arrived at the ER. "What's your birthday? What is your mother's name?"

It took me a second, but the answers came. I put the whole story together for Mom and the doctor.

"I was going to lie there, but a woman called to me. She stayed with me until I was able to get up."

"Who? Was it Gail? Or Mrs. Sunkes?" Mom asked, naming neighbors one by one.

"I didn't recognize her," I said.

"You didn't recognize her?" Mom couldn't understand why a stranger would be walking on Willow Lane. Come to think of it, neither could I. There were no other roads around ours. No sidewalks leading there. The only people who walked on Willow Lane were the people who lived on it. And we knew everyone.

"It's a good thing you didn't just lie there," the doctor said. "You would have fallen asleep with a minor concussion—never a good idea."

When we returned home, I joined my parents on the couch. My dad switched on a movie. I grabbed one of my mother's yarn skeins and rolled it into a ball. We sat quietly, grateful for the calm. *If I didn't see that woman, I might still be out there in the rain,* I thought as I rested my head on my mom's shoulder. But instead I was warm. Safe. Somehow, it had never occurred to me to appreciate that before.

The following morning my mother asked around the neighborhood to find out who had been out walking at twilight, wearing a yellow coat. No one knew what she was talking about. She never found an answer. Turns out, sleepy old Willow Lane had at least one mysterious stranger. And my boring world held a few surprises after all.

Golden Angels
Sidney Usary

AUNT KATHY AND UNCLE RAY waved at my cousin and me as we went up on the ski lift. I was excited to hit the slopes without anyone holding my hand—at ten years old, I was ready to be responsible for myself and seven-year-old Noah. Besides, the bunny slope at Snow Summit was a piece of cake.

I looked around as we climbed. *Strange,* I thought. Did the lift always take this long? Why were so few skiers on it? Finally we reached the top. There was no lift attendant. Only the sign Black Diamond Run. We'd taken the wrong lift!

The lift dumped us onto the snow. We slid down the steep slope, finally stopping at the bottom of a snowbank. Expert skiers jumped over the bank, flying above our heads so fast that they didn't notice us. Noah began to cry.

"God," I pleaded, "help us! We're freezing and we can't get down!"

Just then, we heard the drone of engines. Two snowmobiles zoomed toward us. We were wary of strangers, but the drivers wore gold helmets and gold uniforms with ski patrol insignia. We wrapped our arms around their gold jackets and they raced up the mountain. At the summit, they put us on the ski lift headed down. Then they drove off into the woods.

Aunt Kathy and Uncle Ray brought us into the ski patrol office to thank the unit for sending their "golden angels."

That's when they told us: The official ski patrol uniforms are red.

Angel in a Thunderstorm

Linda Reed as told to Sophy Burnham

LINDA REED AND HER HUSBAND, David, were living in Atlanta, Georgia, when one Fourth of July her mother and sister came to visit. For a treat the family drove to a state park to hike along a verdant stream with its rushing waterfalls. Suddenly, as happens in the mountains, a thunderstorm hit. They ran back to the car in the pelting rain, and while they drove down the zigzag switchbacks, the storm grew worse, with first leaves then twigs then branches blowing across the road in a slashing sideways-slanting rain. Trees were falling. Theirs was the first car to be blocked by a fallen tree across the road, a magnificent maple with half its roots still clawing the earth.

When the others got out in the torrential rain to inspect the tree, Linda's mother stayed in the warm dry car: "I'll just pray," she said with confidence.

The other three, together with passengers from other cars, tugged in vain at the huge tree—as if seven or eight people could hope to move a maple.

Linda returned to the car, wet and chilled. "I'm sorry, Mom," she said. "It looks like we'll be here for a while."

"Oh, don't worry," said her mother. "I'm praying."

A few moments later a man walked out of the woods to their right. He was dressed in a black and red flannel shirt, a cigarette dangling out of his mouth, and in his hand he carried a powered-up chain saw. Silently he cut up the tree. It took about three minutes. Everyone rushed to thank him, even pay him, but as with most angels, he accepted nothing. He walked back into the trees as quickly as he had arrived.

A few weeks later Linda and her husband returned to the same location. It was easy to find because of the chopped-up branches, debris, and the large tree stump, still half-embedded in the earth. They wandered off the road and into the woods looking for a campsite, or cabin, or signs of firewood or logging—anything that might have housed a man with a chain saw on that stormy night. There was nothing.

Going Too Fast

Brenda Boswell

IT WAS RAINING. I WAS driving down a fairly busy retail area street. I was in a hurry to get what I needed and to get home. My mind was roaming when all of a sudden I was at my turn. I was going too fast and my tires were nearly threadbare, yet here I was making an irresponsible turn anyway.

Panic began to set in when I saw I was not going to make the turn but was heading right at a car waiting to pull out on the main road. *Oh, dear God,* my mind was streaking, *I am going to hit this woman and I cannot stop.* I could actually see the terror on her face as I was quickly approaching the driver's side of her car.

I began praying. That was literally all that was left to do. "Dear God, don't let this woman be seriously injured," I prayed. I was braking hard, my tires were sliding on the wet pavement, and I was bearing down on this poor woman with no way out of it. "Dear Lord, protect this woman from my careless, stupid actions. Please. Please. Please," I was shouting to God.

Then in an instant my car (not with any help from me) arched around the corner. We were eyeball-to-eyeball as my car passed hers. I could clearly see the woman's stilled, pale, panicked face. I am pretty sure mine looked the same.

I actually had to pull over off the road and breathe. My mind was searching. What happened? I know that beyond a shadow of a doubt I was going to hit and harm another human being with my bad driving. How on earth did I *not* hit that car?

I believe it was my and probably her guardian angels watching over both of us. I have a long-settled knowing of God's gracious gift of angels to His people. There are so many readings from the Holy Word that absolutely confirm it.

And it is, for me, the only answer for that day's event.

My Two Visitors

Frederick Morris

WHEN I WAS AROUND FIVE years old, my naval officer father returned from sea and our large family piled into our new station wagon and traveled from Norfolk, Virginia, to Sligo, Pennsylvania, to see my grandparents and our extended family. It was Christmastime. I remember being mesmerized by colored lights gracing the houses and trees as we made the long trek.

Soon I'd fallen asleep and was roused from my slumber well past midnight to see we had finally arrived at the old house in the country. There was lots of excitement, hugs, and kisses all around, especially from Gram and Grampa.

Later after things settled and everyone had gone to sleep, I had to use the bathroom and suddenly realized I didn't know the way. I recalled my mother telling us that the bathrooms weren't working because of the construction going on in the house and that my grandfather and uncle had dug an outhouse near the garage. I fumbled around in the dark and found my way down the stairs.

But when I got to the door that would take me outside, I stopped. I was paralyzed by the darkness and the unknown. For a moment, I stood wondering what to do. It was too late to wake anyone or ask for help.

In desperation, I asked God to help me find my way. I opened the back door, stepped into the cold night, and looked up at the sky. In the deep country darkness, the stars appeared grander, brighter, and infinitely greater in number than I'd ever seen before. But even the brightness of the stars didn't aid my plight. I had no idea how to find the outhouse. I said another quick prayer, and then I heard someone behind me. I turned to see my great-aunt Bernie. Seeing her familiar, kindly face immediately put me at ease.

"Come on, Freddy," she said. "I'll show you the way." She took my hand and led me down a path that appeared to be a construction site just inches from the door. Ahead, I saw the narrow outhouse with its funny-looking door, and Aunt Bernie led me there.

I entered the small building. There was no light, so I made the best of the situation. When I had finished, I opened the door to find Aunt Bernie waiting not far off. I stepped outside the shack, took her hand again, and she led me back into the house. I climbed the stairs to my room and promptly fell asleep.

The next morning I entered the kitchen to find many family members gathered. My grandmother stood at the oven cooking, and family members sat in the kitchen, drinking coffee as they reminisced and caught up on one another's lives.

I grabbed something to eat and had just sat down when my cousin Charlie came over to say hello. Charlie was just a few years older than I was, and he was a handsome, confident boy with blond hair and twinkling blue eyes. Charlie had always taken me under his wing whenever our families got together, and perhaps because of this, he was the subject of much hero worship from me. I was so excited to see him, and I started telling him about what had happened the night before. Everything was fine until I mentioned that Aunt Bernie had guided me to the outhouse.

He turned pale, and an odd expression crossed his face.

"Are you sure?" he asked me.

"Yes," I told him. "It was late and I was worried, but she told me everything would be okay and showed me how to find the outhouse."

"Show me," he replied, looking serious.

I opened the door and stepped back. To my shock, the area in front of the door looked nothing like what I had seen the night before. If I had stood where I thought I had, I would have fallen into a deep hole and surely would have been injured or worse.

"But it can't be! I'm sure that's where Aunt Bernie took me."

"Are you sure?" he asked me again.

"Yes! How would I have…"

My cousin took me aside and said, "Freddy, listen. I wouldn't tell anyone that story if I were you. It would just upset everyone. Aunt Bernie died last month. She was almost ninety years old."

So I never told. But it was not the last time I would have such an encounter, and my cousin Charlie would once again play a part in it.

Years would pass before I made my way back to Sligo. I had graduated from college and was working in Washington, DC. I rented a small hunting cabin not far from town. I had taken a short leave from my job to recover from a recent breakup of a promising relationship, which had left me depressed and defeated—made worse by the fact that Christmas was approaching. I prayed that this retreat would help me get through this difficult time.

I'd just put a log on the fire the first night, put on the coffee, and settled in, when I heard a gentle knock at the door. It was after midnight, so I approached the door with some trepidation. No one knew I was in town or at the cabin. The only person I'd told was Gram, who was quite elderly by this time, and I was pretty sure was not out this late in the snow.

I opened the door and found a tall man with blond hair and twinkling blue eyes standing in front of me. "Freddy, is that you?"

I studied him. The person standing in front of me reminded me of someone I'd known long before but hadn't seen in years. "Charlie!"

"Hey," he said. "What are you doing out here alone?"

I invited him in and told him about the reasons for coming to the cabin. At that moment, I remembered telling him about the time I saw our aunt Bernie, and a strange feeling flitted over me. I offered him some coffee, and we sat in front of the fire together, talking about old times, catching up, and enjoying the company. As we talked, I felt the weight of a broken heart begin to lift.

After some time, he told me he needed to go, and as he stood, he pressed something into my hand—a picture of him with me and Gram, taken when he and I were still quite young. "I want you to have this." With that, we said our good-byes and promised to keep in touch, and he left.

It was almost morning before I struggled off to bed, bleary-eyed and exhausted but with spirits lifted by my cousin's surprise visit.

That week went by faster than I expected. The time away *had* been just what I needed. I packed and got ready to return to the city. But first I made a detour to my grandmother's house.

"How was your time at the cabin?" Gram asked.

"It was perfect," I told her. "The big surprise this week was that Charlie stopped by to see me."

"What do you mean, honey? Charlie who?"

"Cousin Charlie. He stopped by last week when I was at the cabin. It's amazing how much seeing him took my mind off my troubles, and—"

My grandmother interrupted me. "You know, Freddy, if I were you, I'd not tell anybody that story. I'd just keep it to myself."

She gave me a strange look and then added, "Well, you see, Freddy, Charlie died in a car accident two weeks before you came up to stay at the cabin."

"Gram," I said incredulously. Our extended family was not always good with communication, but I was surprised no one had told me. "But it was definitely Charlie. Look. He gave me this." I handed her the photo of her with Charlie and me.

"Well, now, isn't that something." Gram gave me an odd look as she handed the photo back to me. "Now, who did you say gave you that?"

"Gram, really, it was Charlie."

She walked over to the end table where she kept her scrapbooks, pulled out a blue scrapbook, opened it, and pointed to an empty space in it. "See that? That's where that picture was all these years after it was taken. I put it there myself. Charlie came by about a month or so ago on his way to DC. We talked for a while and had coffee, and I gave him that photo."

I was struck by the coincidence. I was driving back to DC that night just as Charlie was going to do the month before. "Suppose we put that photo back where it belongs," Gram suggested, pointing to the vacant space in the scrapbook. "I'll keep it and you can come take a look at it whenever you're here."

I agreed. We put it back into the photo book. I finished my coffee, kissed Gram, and jumped back in my car.

Sometime later I received a birthday card from Gram. When I opened the envelope, a photo slipped out. It was the photo we'd returned to the scrapbook together. The note in the card read, "Best you have this now." A few weeks later Gram passed away at the age of ninety-two.

I've never seen Aunt Bernie or Charlie again, but during the toughest times of my life, the memories of my visits from them have comforted me and reminded me that we're never alone. God sent help in a form that was comforting and familiar, in answer to the desperate prayers of a frightened young boy and a defeated young man.

No Such Nurse!

Sue Bryson

WHEN MY HUSBAND, JOHNNY, ENTERED a hospital in Houston, Texas, two large aneurysms pressed on his heart and spinal cord. Johnny was scared and uncertain. The surgery might leave him paralyzed, and he didn't want to live as an invalid. We prayed for God's guidance in this decision. Finally Johnny asked me to leave for a while so he could think.

I went to get a cup of coffee with my brother Jack, who had come with us. "Without that operation," I told him, "Johnny probably won't live out the year."

When Jack and I returned an hour later, Johnny was alone in his room, smiling. "You have to meet my nurse, Shu-Lin," he said. "She has convinced me to have the operation."

Shu-Lin had assured Johnny he was in good hands, and promised to pray for him. "Not to worry," she had said.

How had she given my husband confidence when the doctors and I couldn't? "You'll understand when you see her smile," Johnny said.

Jack and I met Shu-Lin later that afternoon. She was everything Johnny had described—Asian in appearance, warm, caring, and cheerful, with a radiant smile.

Johnny's sister Jane arrived to be with us for the surgery, and we went to the waiting room. Shu-Lin accompanied Johnny into surgery. It was her day off, but she said she wanted to be there. During the operation, she returned periodically to let us know how Johnny was doing. Each time she appeared, we felt relief and optimism. Finally the surgery was over, and Shu-Lin came to give us the good news even before the doctor reported to us.

Johnny spent the next five days in intensive care. Often he woke up to find Shu-Lin wiping his forehead or holding his hand. When he was out of danger, Shu-Lin came to say good-bye. "I must go now," she said. "Others need me."

The following week, Johnny was well enough to go home. We decided I should find Shu-Lin to thank her for being so kind. But when I inquired about her, the nurses on duty just looked at me. They had never heard of her. Johnny and Jack and Jane and I knew she had been with us. I went to the administration office, determined to locate Shu-Lin. But I was told there was no such employee.

At that moment I realized: Hospitals don't keep records of guardian angels.

Island of Peace

Joan Wester Anderson

THERE IS A STORY TOLD by a pediatric nurse serving in Danzig in 1945, after Russian troops had overrun many German towns. Local women were being abused, and nights were filled with terror. Nurses gathered as many women and children as they could, and found temporary lodging in a small makeshift school. The nurses often worked at night and, because of the lack of electricity, used candle stubs.

Since theirs was the only lighted building, they, too, faced the danger of being invaded by the Russians. Yet the people called this building the "island of peace" because despite the surroundings, nothing bad ever seemed to happen there. Gradually the stream of those seeking shelter increased.

One day a woman brought her children and begged the nurses to take them. The children had had a completely secular upbringing and had never heard of prayer. That evening, as the community held a worship service, instead of folding his hands with the rest, the new boy stared into the distance with wide eyes. At the end, the community sang a familiar song, asking God to send angels to "place golden weapons around our beds."

"When we said 'Amen,' the boy came up to me and drew me out of the building," the nurse reported. "He kept tapping his breastbone and saying, 'Up to here. It came up to here on them.'"

The nurse asked him what he meant. Pointing up to the gutter on the roof of the building, he repeated his statement: "The gutter came up to here on them."

"What are you talking about?" the nurse asked.

The boy told her that while everyone had been singing, he had seen men ablaze with lights at every corner of the building. The men were so tall that they towered above the roof, their arms outstretched over everyone in the little structure.

"Now it was clear to me," the nurse noted. "We had not seen them, but they certainly were watching us. This house could be called the 'island of peace' because angels guarded it all."

Sheltered by His Wings

Edna Yvonne James

I WOULD WAIT UP FOR my mother, Mary Hampton Battle, to come home from work, for most of my teenage years. She was one of the two night custodians at Garrison Elementary School in Centreville, Illinois, a school in our neighborhood, right outside of East St. Louis.

I liked to make sure the fire was still going and the house was warm when she came in about ten or eleven o'clock. We would have a snack and chat together before going to bed. My mother was a very spiritual woman with a strong faith in God, and I loved our late-night routine. It was our special time, my time alone with her while my three brothers and two sisters slept.

One night my mother came in from work with an amazing story that stays with me still.

She and her coworker, Mrs. Alexander, were well into their evening routine of sweeping, dusting, and general cleaning of each classroom of Garrison Elementary School. They had gone to the third floor and were starting to mop the hallways and stairwell down to the first floor. Big windows in the stairwell looked out onto inky darkness. The occasional dim sound of a car broke the song of crickets. The old three-story school was set back from the street—like the church across the road, which, of course, was empty during the night when my momma worked.

"I was mopping the second-floor hallway when I heard a *clank* and some voices right outside," my mother told me. "I thought it was someone messing with my car—maybe trying to pry the hood open and steal the car battery."

My mom was a real take-charge kind of person. I knew she would not be afraid to go downstairs, poke her head out of the door, and yell, "Get away from here!" She began to walk toward the stairwell. But before she could take more than a few steps down the stairs, she came to a sudden stop.

There, on the landing, was an angel blocking her way. It was a tall being— about seven feet tall, dressed in white clothing. It hovered in midair with its wings spread, without saying a word.

"I looked straight at the angel," my mother told me. "His face was kind and loving, like the pictures of Jesus you see hanging on a wall."

The sight of an angel startled her, but she knew to respect God's work. Because she did not know why it was there, she continued to mop the second-floor hallway. When she finished, the angel was gone and she proceeded downstairs, where she told Mrs. Alexander what she had seen. They both wondered if the angel was a sign.

Later, when they were ready to go home, they walked out together and discovered that someone had been tampering with my mother's car. My momma realized that had she gone out when she first heard the noise, she might have been injured or killed. "I knew that angel was there for protection."

"You know that song our church choir sings? 'All night, all day, angels keep watching over me,'" my mother softly sang. "That happened to me. God watched over me tonight."

Mom, I Saw an Angel

Guadalupe C. Casillas

SOMETHING WAS DIFFERENT ONE PARTICULAR night. As one of my sons, Ed, slept, I heard his labored breathing. That had never occurred before. He didn't have a cold, allergies, or asthma. He had been perfectly well the entire day and during our story time.

It was bedtime. Before ten-year-old Ed fell asleep, he listened as I read him one of the stories from his children's Bible.

It was a special time to tuck him in and tell him about God, as well as stories about insects and reptiles. After reading, I turned out the light. As I snuggled next to Ed, we talked until he fell asleep—a precious way to end the day.

As he slept next to me on that particular night, I heard an unfamiliar, strange sound. It was his breathing—it was different. All kinds of thoughts invaded my mind. *Is he sick... Will he stop breathing during the night and die?* My overprotective motherly instincts took over my heart and mind. I considered spending the entire night next to him to monitor his breathing.

Should I wake him up and take him to the emergency room? I stayed a few more minutes to see if his condition would improve, but it didn't get any better or worse. Was I overreacting?

Lord, I don't know what's going on with Ed, but I know You'll take care of him even if I don't stay next to him. Father, there isn't much I can do to help him. I'm going to trust You and go to my bed. I know there will be times when I can't always be with him. But this I know, You will always be with him and watch over him.

I left my son's room to lie next to my husband. Confident that God would take care of Ed, I felt God's peace and I fell asleep right away.

The next morning, my youngest son, Andrew, rushed downstairs to eat his cereal before school. Ed also ran down the stairs to have his favorite cereal.

"It's time to brush your teeth and get dressed, boys. Come on, we don't want to be late to school," I said.

We made it on time to school. I went on my daily routine to clean the house and run my usual errands. The hours flew during the morning, and it was soon time to pick up the boys from school. I waited in the parking lot for my sons to approach the car. The usual conversation started.

"How was your day?"

"Good."

"Did you have a good time? What did you learn? Are you hungry?"

Then in the middle of our conversation Ed said, "Mom, I saw an angel last night."

"You mean, you dreamt of an angel, right?"

"No, Mom. I saw one."

"What do you mean?"

My son told me that he had awakened in the middle of the night struggling to breathe. I then remembered how worried I had been about his breathing.

"Go on…"

"Mom, I was scared. I couldn't breathe. All of a sudden, I saw a bright light in my room. Then I saw the angel and he told me, 'Do not be afraid, for the Lord is with you.'"

"What did he look like, Ed?"

"He had a long white robe."

"Did you see his face?"

"No. The light was too bright."

"You said he talked to you…What did his voice sound like?"

"Soothing…like rushing waters. Oh, Mom, he also said he was the angel of the Lord. He had a golden sash around his waist."

The Angel of the Lord? Could it be? The Bible refers to Jesus as the Angel of the Lord…Was Jesus the One who came to his rescue? Now it was my breathing that became different. I held my breath and my eyes grew wide.

"What happened next?" I asked.

"I was not afraid, Mom. My breathing was normal, and I went back to sleep."

"Ed, last night after you fell asleep, you were breathing kind of strange. I didn't know whether I should stay with you the whole night or not. I prayed for God to protect you even if I wasn't there to watch over you."

My fears had been real after all. My son's breathing had actually become worse and he had struggled for air. Amazed by God's love and protection, I asked Ed, "Did you know that when the Bible speaks of the 'Angel of the Lord' it's referring to Jesus?" His eyes locked into my eyes as we both contemplated what had occurred. Joyfully I said, "Ed, I believe it was Jesus Who came to help you." My son was elated with this wonderful experience, and he told his dad and my family about it.

I thanked God for watching over Ed. This tangible moment has kept the heart of an overprotective mother at peace over all these years. God will always be with my son—wherever he is.

Ed is now thirty years old. One afternoon as we went out to lunch he was consumed with overwhelming thoughts about his future. I reminded him about his childhood encounter with Jesus when he struggled to breathe and that He was still here to also lead him by the hand to face the challenges of this life.

"Mom, so many years have gone by, I've wondered if it was only a dream."

"I know it wasn't a dream, Ed. You know how I know this? Your abnormal breathing worried me and it caused me to ask God to protect you. Plus, how could you at ten years of age know Jesus has a golden sash around His waist? I didn't know that either. Months later after you shared your encounter with me, as I read my Bible, I came across this passage: 'And among the lampstands was someone like a son of man, dressed in a robe reaching down to his feet and with a golden sash around his chest' (Revelation 1:13, NIV). So I looked up the word *sash* and found this other verse in Isaiah 11:5 (NIV): 'Righteousness will be his belt and faithfulness the sash around his waist.'"

My son then realized it had not been a dream. Jesus had heard the prayer of a mother who knew that even though she wasn't physically with her son, God would be there. I know through God's Word that God is always in control and that He watches over my sons. He ordained their days before even one of them yet came to be.

Ask for Woody

Mildred V. Carroll

MY BEST FRIEND, MERIETHA, CALLED just before five. "There's a big sale at Macy's," she said. "I'll meet you at the subway after work." I wasn't in the mood for an excursion all the way from Brooklyn, New York, into Manhattan, but Merietha was partially paralyzed on her left side, and though she got around well with her cane, it was easier for her to move through the throngs of shoppers with my help.

By the time we were done at Macy's it was after nine. The subway wasn't the best place at night for two ladies bogged down with packages, so we decided to take it only as far as a stop where we could transfer to a bus to Brooklyn. Still, I was worried. I prayed as we got on the train, *Lord, help us have a safe trip home.*

When we pulled into a station on the Lower East Side, Merietha gathered her bags and headed for the doors. "I think our stop is the next one," I said tentatively.

"No, this is it," she insisted. As soon as we got up to the street, I knew we were in the wrong place. Not a soul was in sight. Peering around the corner, I spotted a bus stop beneath a lamppost about five blocks away.

We started in that direction. Then, from out of the darkness, a voice called, "Mrs. Carroll!" A young man I had never seen before came up to us.

"Mrs. Carroll," he said, "what are you two doing out here at this time of night? It's not safe."

I glanced at his shabby jeans and T-shirt. "Do I know you?" I asked, hoping my voice sounded steady. When I felt Merietha's grip on my arm tighten, I looked at the man more closely. I couldn't help but notice his deep brown eyes, which seemed full of concern and compassion.

"Where are you from?" I asked. He walked along with us, going slowly so Merietha could keep up, but didn't offer any information about himself.

Near the bus stop a group of surly-looking people blocked our path. They glared menacingly, but our companion remained calm. "Hi, folks," he said. "These ladies are with me." They let us pass.

The bus came, and the young man rode with us back to Brooklyn. Before we said good-bye, I gave him my phone number. "Stay in touch," I urged. "I'd like to keep you in my prayers."

He smiled. "Ask for Woody," he said, handing me his number.

The next day I called to thank him properly. "This is a boardinghouse," the person who answered told me. "No one by that name lives here."

Then where had Woody come from? Suddenly I knew. After all, hadn't I asked the Lord to help us get home safely?

CHAPTER 4

Angels from the Realms of Glory

Field of Dreams

Katherine Dean

LAST THING I REMEMBERED WAS driving home with my mother. Now I was surrounded by twisted metal and broken glass. *We've had an accident*, I thought. *I must have passed out.* I tried to get up. Pain shot through my body.

I looked outside the car and saw a sunny green field alive with vibrant yellow buttercups. I felt a pair of hands gently push me back into my seat, but I didn't see anyone. "Lie back," a voice said. "It's not your time to go to the field yet." I passed out again.

My husband, Jimmie, was by my side when I woke up again in the hospital, in a full body cast. The doctor explained that I'd been unconscious for three days. "It was critical that you didn't move before the EMTs arrived," he said.

Jimmie waited until we were alone, and then leaned in close. "I'm sorry," he whispered. "Your mother didn't survive."

I thought back to the details of that day. The comforting hands, the sunny green field full of buttercups. "When I tried to get out of the car someone kept me safe," I told Jimmie. "A field of buttercups off the side of the road looked like a heavenly landscape in bright, glorious sunlight."

Jimmie shook his head. "No, honey. The car went off the road by a cornfield. And it was raining."

Jimmie showed me newspaper articles about the accident. The photographs proved him right: Mother and I had been hit head-on near a cornfield on a rainy day. But how had I seen that sunlit vision of buttercups? Whose invisible hands had guided me back into my seat?

Perhaps I've been given a glimpse of Mother's heavenly home. Surely the angel who kept me safe guided her into that glorious field.

Hospice Deepened My Faith

Michael W. Elmore

AS A HOSPICE CHAPLAIN, I'VE been present as hundreds of people have transitioned from their final moments of life. Not all transitions are remarkable. Some are peaceful; everyone's passage is different. However, as I have accompanied people through their final journey, certain individuals have left me with an indelible belief that heaven is a real place.

For example, Rose was a prim and genteel woman with a sense of pleasure for the finer things in life. I was surprised when I first met her because she had brought many of her cherished belongings and transformed her austere hospice room into the familiar surroundings of home.

During one of my visits, Rose glanced at the corner of her room repeatedly. She seemed to be looking at something, and she asked me to look, as well. "Do you see him?" she asked.

"See whom?"

"The angel who watches over me."

I stared but saw nothing. Each time I visited, Rose talked about the sense of peace she felt because of the angelic visitations. Many patients in hospice experience surges of anxiety, but not Rose. I believe the day Rose slipped from this life into something more, she was borne on an angel's wings, peacefully and comfortably. Rose's sense of serenity left a lasting impression that deepened my belief in heaven.

Angels Ever Near

Michael W. Elmore

MARC CAME TO HOSPICE IN the final stage of cancer. He brought along his yellow Labrador named Jake, whom the vet also diagnosed with cancer.

Marc insisted that Jake share his bed so the longtime friends could spend their last days together. When I asked Marc about his final wishes, he shared two things with me. First, he wanted to have a few photos taken with Jake as a keepsake for his family. Second, he wished that Jake would die before him so that his dog wouldn't have to bear the weight of separation from his master.

After I shared Marc's final wishes with our social worker, she took several snapshots of Jake resting on Marc's lap in "their" hospice bed. The next day, Jake died. Marc said good-bye to his friend of many years, sad but relieved that his Lab had passed away. Comforted by Jake's passing, Marc relaxed and let go of his own ebbing life. Before the photos could be developed, Marc was gone, as well.

A few days later, Marc's pictures came back from the photo lab. When we gathered around and opened the envelope, someone gasped. I looked over the shoulder of one of the nurses and saw a most unusual thing. Around Marc's bed appeared a luminescent circle of tall angelic beings surrounding him and Jake.

It was obvious that these photos were not some developer's careless mistake. They were the angelic forms present at Marc's bedside, fulfilling their watchful duty of waiting for the time of Jake's and Marc's passings. A sense of awe spread over me.

I'm convinced that heaven is a real place. My patients' experiences have proven it to me.

Angelic Trio

David Michael Smith

"DON'T YOU SEE THEM? THEY'RE right there, in the corner." My father, Bob Smith, was dying from lung cancer that had spread throughout most of his failing, aged body. The ravaging cancer cells had left him paralyzed from the waist down and imprisoned by a lonely hospice bed in his home. My mother, Phyllis, assisted the hospice nurses the best she could, but mostly she just loved on Dad and listened to him.

"Where? I don't see anything," she replied, looking into the corner of the room where Dad's eyes seemed to focus.

"They're there, smiling at me. Three immaculately dressed men...angels," he whispered in awe. Mom looked again, but she saw nothing.

Dad started smoking at the age of twelve in Knoxville, Tennessee, his hometown, mostly because all of his friends smoked. He grew up in tobacco country, where it was commonplace and accepted. His smoking grew into an adulthood addiction he couldn't defeat until at the age of fifty-three, for no explainable reason, he went cold turkey. Like many others who quit, he replaced one habit with another to satisfy his cravings—Life Savers candy. Dad went through one to two packs of Life Savers daily, usually Wild Cherry or Mint-O-Green flavored. He gained some weight and looked healthier than ever.

Twenty years later, the effect of years of inhaling nicotine and carcinogens snuck up on him, and he battled for his life. With his lungs shot, he could barely breathe even with an oxygen respirator.

I visited the day after his heavenly vision and sat at his bedside to talk. Soft Christmas carols played in the background. It was November, and we played the carols because we knew it was unlikely Dad would survive to experience the holiday season.

"Mom says you saw three angels yesterday, Dad," I said.

"It wasn't the first time," he said. "They've visited several times, three well-dressed men, perfect, pressed suits, always smiling. I know they're angels and they're assigned to take me home."

"I've heard people see loved ones, angels, all kinds of things when the end is near," I answered, not sure what to say. "Do they ever talk to you?"

"Your mother doesn't see or hear them. I guess it's one of those unexplainable, death things, but, yes, they talk." I waited for him to tell me more.

"They tell me it's going to be okay, that I don't have much more time, and that great joy and love are waiting for me," he said with wet, foggy eyes. "I've never known such peace as when they're around. Perfect peace, son, perfect peace…"

Several days later, the family gathered around Dad's bed and prayed. We said our tearful good-byes, kissed his forehead, and held his hands. He was unconscious, barely holding on. We told him it was all right for him to leave us and to go with his three angels heavenward. It was a poignant moment to watch a dear loved one about to die in our presence. Memories of my father began to roll across the movie screen of my mind, and I shed unashamed tears.

Dad exhaled his final gasp of earthly breath, and then he was gone. That afternoon the family made funeral plans, called relatives and church members, and began phase one of adjusting to life without Bob Smith in the world… our world.

I hugged my mother and left to join my wife and young daughter at home.

As the sun was preparing to set that night, I went out to walk my dog, Buddy Bear, and prayed for a sign—any sign—that Dad was indeed with his Savior and Creator. I was hurting inside, pretending to be strong, but really struggling. I needed something—anything—from above.

Seconds after I prayed, I looked up. Out of a cloudless November blue sky, three birds appeared on the horizon and flew directly toward me. They descended at a rapid rate and zipped over me with flapping wings. I actually ducked a bit, afraid they might graze the top of my head.

Just then, I noticed a fourth bird behind them—a little smaller—and it joined the trio. As I spun around to watch, they ascended, in beautiful aerodynamic formation, higher and higher until they were out of sight. Everything was quiet again.

For me, that was an answer to prayer. Others may not see it that way, and that's all right. I know God gave me the sign I asked for: the four birds. Dad and his three escorting angels.

A Glimpse of Eternity

Catherine Marshall

ONE OCTOBER, IN THE LIVING room of our Virginia farm, I heard this extraordinary adventure from a woman named Betty Malz. Many are going to find the facts of her story difficult to believe. It's a story I can vouch for.

The adventure began one June night in 1959. Betty, twenty-nine; her husband, John, a salesman for the Sun Oil company in Indiana; their daughter, Brenda; Betty's parents, the Glenn Perkinses; and her little brother had just arrived for a two-week family vacation at Gulf Vista Retreat, Florida. They spent that first day swimming, waterskiing, surfing, and shell-hunting. Exhausted, Betty and her husband went to bed early.

Then the pain began. Hand pressed on her stomach, Betty Malz first wondered, *What did I eat for dinner?* Then as the pain increased, she thought, *What a way to start our vacation!* Finally Betty turned on the light and woke her husband. When the pain became excruciating, he drove her to the hospital.

Betty lay in the hospital several days while the doctors made dozens of tests and debated her situation. Finally she was sent by plane to a hospital in her hometown of Terre Haute, Indiana, where on the eleventh day of her illness, she was operated on by a gynecologist-surgeon. He found an appendix long-ruptured, with a huge mass of gangrene in her abdomen. Every organ was coated.

"I can give you no hope," the surgeon told her husband and her parents. "I've lost two-hundred-pound men in forty-eight hours with a fraction of the gangrene we have here. She can live only a few hours."

But Betty did not die that night, nor the next. In fact, on the fourth day she lapsed into a coma. She was to be in that coma for most of the next month.

The days passed. Ten. Twenty. Betty was given multiple blood transfusions and intravenous feedings. Not a mouthful of food passed her lips. Meanwhile, two more operations followed.

More days passed—twenty-five, thirty. The doctors were certain that the comatose patient could see or hear nothing.

"That was not the case," Betty said. "All that time that I was a prisoner of my own body, when I couldn't speak, see, or smell, or control the movement of a muscle, I could hear everything the doctors, nurses, and visitors said. It was as though when my physical senses went, all spiritual senses were sharpened. If people came into my room feeling hopeless about me, I knew it. When they had faith that I would get well, I knew that, and it helped me. If only people could realize," Betty said with great emphasis, "that in any form of unconsciousness or coma—even under anesthetics, I do believe—unerringly the spirit picks up those attitudes."

On July 31, Betty's fever shot still higher as pneumonia set in. Then her veins collapsed completely; no more transfusions or intravenous feedings were possible.

"The battle is lost," the exhausted family was told. "You'd better get some rest. We'll call you if there's any change."

Sadly Betty's husband drove home and her parents drove the thirty-one miles to their home in Clay City. At 2:30 the next morning, Betty's father, Mr. Perkins, was sharply awakened—he did not know how. He had a strong compulsion to get to the hospital immediately. He resisted at first. Finally he gave in, dressed, and was on his way shortly after 4:00 AM.

Sometime after he had left the house, the telephone rang. It was a nurse calling. "Mrs. Perkins, I'm so sorry to have to give you this message. Your daughter Betty expired a few minutes ago." There was a pause. "I've already called her husband, of course. He will be coming over as soon as possible this morning."

Concern for her own husband temporarily overcame Mrs. Perkins's anguished grief. "But my husband is already on his way there. Please have someone watch for him and intercept him. It would be a dreadful shock for him to walk into Betty's room and find her."

The nurse promised—and hung up.

"I got there and walked down the hospital corridor. Everything seemed too quiet, too deserted," Betty's father told me. "I remember how my heart skipped a beat as I rounded the corner...stood in the doorway...saw the still form on the bed. Betty was covered with a sheet. Every bit of apparatus had been removed, all instruments; even the chart was gone.

"I was stunned and despairing. I couldn't even pray. I could only stand by the bed softly crying, 'Jesus! Jesus!'"

How could the sorrowing man possibly have known the extraordinary adventure his daughter was experiencing at that moment? Let Betty tell it:

"I was walking up a steep hill. Yet there was no muscular exertion, it was more like a light skipping or floating movement, without effort. I thought, *Why, steep hills have always affected the muscles in the calves of my legs.* There was none of that—all movement was a delight. The grass under my feet was a vivid green and of a velvety texture, yet every blade seemed alive.

"To my right was a high silvery marble wall. To the left, slightly behind me, was a tall angel. I could see only his feet as he walked, and the bottom of his garment swaying as in a gentle breeze. In the near distance were the echoes of multitudes of voices singing, worshipping Jesus.

"As the angel and I reached the top of the hill, I saw tall ornate gates, the tops of a scroll-like Gothic design. The gates had a translucent quality like pearl. There were no handles, no way I could have opened them. The angel stepped forward and pressed his palms against the gate.

"I stood there for what seemed like a long time, reveling in the wonderful music. The feel of beauty was everywhere. From time to time I would sing along with the voices in the distance. I remember two of the songs—old, old hymns: "For I Have Been Born Again" and "The Old Account Was Settled Long Ago." Finally the angel spoke. 'Would you like to enter and sing with them?'

"I answered, 'No, I would like to stand here and sing awhile, then go back to my family.'

"The angel nodded. I sensed that the choice was mine. Then I was coming back down the grassy slope, and the sun was on my left coming up over the wall. I remember noticing details like the sharp shadow of the beautiful gates on the wall."

It was at that moment that the world of spirit and this world of time and space fused back together for Betty. In her room the sun was also coming up. Under the sheet Betty began to feel the rising sun warming her cold body.

Despite the sheet over her head, Betty saw moving, wavy letters about two inches high go before her like a ticker-tape message on the sunbeams. She has no idea whether she was "seeing" with her spiritual eyes or with her physical eyes. After what she had experienced on the grassy slope, she knew that the one is as real as the other.

"The letters," Betty told me, "seemed composed of translucent ivory, only fluid—moving through the rays of the sun. They stretched all the way from the window, past my bed, on into the room, and read, 'I am the resurrection, and the life: he that believeth in me, though he were dead, yet shall he live' (John 11:25, KJV).

"The words were so alive that they pulsated. I knew that I had to touch those living words. When I, by faith, reached up to grasp the words, I pushed the sheet off my face. At that instant the Word literally became life to me; the warmth in the moving letters flowed into my fingers and up my arm. I sat up in bed. I was alive!"

At first Betty did not notice her father standing beside her; she had eyes only for the unearthly light in the room and she began to search for its source. Her first awareness was of the vivid greenness of the grass on the hospital lawn—*So beautiful!* she thought—and of a man carrying on his shoulder a case of 7UP into the building. Into Betty's heart welled a great love for that man. Then, at last, she noticed her father by her bed.

He was standing there stunned, too stunned to cry out or to hug her ecstatically or to shed tears of joy. Rather, he was rooted to the spot, struck dumb with awe before the majesty of the working of God Himself.

His second reaction was a consuming curiosity to know what Betty had seen. For most of the experience taking place before his eyes had been veiled from him. "Betty, Betty, tell me. What's been going on? Describe it," he ordered, completely forgetting that his daughter had not spoken in weeks.

Nurses and doctors streamed in and out, asking questions. There had been no breathing, no heartbeat, no blood pressure. Between twenty and thirty minutes had elapsed between the telephone call to Mrs. Perkins and the moment Betty had sat up in bed. Now everybody wanted to see Betty, wanted to hear the story from her own lips. When Betty's own doctor kept shaking his head in disbelief, she would look at him in astonishment. "But I'm alive. I can talk and see and smell and feel. I feel fine." That night Betty had a sound sleep.

The next day the doctor closed Betty's door, pulled up a chair, and sat by the bed holding her hand. He spoke softly, his voice kind. "There are some medical facts I must help you face," he began gravely. "You may have a hard life ahead of you. Peritonitis and gangrene have caused a disintegration of the organs of your body. You may have to wear a bag on your side for elimination. In my opinion, you must never try to have another child."

The doctor went on to warn Betty that she had been blind for weeks and should be ready for this to recur. Further, so many heavy narcotics had been administered that there was every likelihood of a severe withdrawal problem.

Betty lay there letting the grim words pour over her, but somehow they didn't penetrate. "I certainly want to be realistic," she told the kind doctor. She had always prided herself on being a down-to-earth person, but now, the knowledge of that other world—so beautiful, so solid, where everything is right, so close at hand—lingered and would not be denied. Deep within her was the assurance that God "hath done all things well" (Mark 7:37, KJV).

Over sixteen years have gone by. Betty never had to wear a bag. Her eyesight has been better than ever.

"And any other baby you have might well be deformed," the doctor had said. Sitting there in the living room at our farm, instinctively Betty's eyes, and mine, went to her delightful daughter April, who was romping in the yard outside. Nothing ethereal or otherworldly about this healthy little girl. Her mother's joy in life is clearly reflected in her.

Great as the physical miracle for Betty is, much greater still are the gifts and graces that have accompanied it. Among them, a new appreciation for life itself, a new love for people. "I had to 'die' to learn how to live," she told me. "God had to take my life away long enough to teach me how to use it. Best of all, now I know there's nothing at all to fear in death. It's simply changing locations."

On a Butterfly Wing

Eben Alexander III, MD

I'VE BEEN A NEUROSURGEON FOR more than twenty years. Over that time, I've heard a lot about angels. Angels who have shown up in patients' recovery rooms after a rough surgery, angels who come in dreams to comfort friends of a patient, and angels who visit mourning relatives. Angels who always seem extraordinarily real to the people who see them. Such people cite convincing details about their angel's appearance, so the angels don't seem vague or imaginary at all.

I listened to these stories with sympathy. Neurosurgeons deal with the brain, the single most complex, and least understood, organ in the body. Operating on the brain can be highly traumatic both for patients and their loved ones. So I'd nod my head and say that such blessed events could happen.

Not that I believed any of these angels were real. The brain is a fantastically efficient machine—efficient enough that if traumatized by illness or surgery, it can actually fool itself into getting better by generating healing imagery. Imagery like a guardian angel, complete with white robes and wings and whatever else a patient might find most comforting. When patients experienced angelic visitations like this, they were simply benefiting from the marvelously efficient mechanisms that the brain possesses that allow it to automatically soothe and heal itself.

Of course, I never said any of this to my patients. These kinds of experiences can be hugely helpful. It was not my place to burst the bubble of a patient who wanted to believe in angels. If it helped a patient get better, then she could believe in anything she wanted.

So you can imagine my surprise when, during the week beginning the tenth of November 2008, I encountered my own guardian angel.

I awoke in my wife Holley's and my Lynchburg, Virginia, house an hour earlier than usual, with a nasty backache. Thinking it was leftover from the low-grade flu that Holley, our younger son, Bond, and I had been suffering from all week, I tiptoed down to the bathroom and ran a hot tub.

The hot water only made the pain worse. It spread to my head. I managed to get myself back to bed. I flopped facedown beside Holley, and she woke up and asked me what was wrong. A little later Bond awoke and came in, as well. Hearing that I had a headache, he reached out and massaged my temples gently.

I screamed in agony. Holley wanted to call an ambulance, but I told her the pain would go away on its own. "Trust me," I said. "I'm a doctor."

Holley left me to rest quietly for a while and got Bond ready for school. She stayed out of the room for an hour and a half so as not to wake me. When she finally came back in, she found me lying rigid on the bed, my jaw jutting forward, my eyes rolled back in my head. I was having a full grand mal seizure, a type of seizure that affects the entire brain.

Holley called for an ambulance, and forty-five minutes later I was wheeled into Lynchburg General Hospital, where I'd worked for years. By that afternoon, I'd slid deep into a coma: one from which I would not recover for another seven days. My doctors discovered that I'd contracted a disease, very rare in adults, called bacterial meningitis. Millions of E. coli bacteria had invaded my brain and spinal cord, and were literally eating my cortex—the outermost portion of the brain, and the part responsible for nearly everything that makes us human. Thought, logic, emotion…it all comes from the cortex. By that Monday afternoon, mine was completely shut down with very, very little likelihood of it working ever again. My chances of survival were small. My chances of surviving as anything more than a vegetable, essentially nonexistent.

Family and friends gathered at the hospital, and over the next seven days they kept a vigil at my bedside, praying for my recovery. For the first few days my doctors tried to stay hopeful. By day five, none of them believed I stood a chance of surviving. So on day seven, they met with Holley and gave her the news that no doctor ever wants to have to deliver.

It was time to take me off life support—to let me die.

Just a room away, I lay in the position I had lain in all week—a ventilator tube down my throat, my face slack, my hands and feet beginning to curl up like leaves as my circulation gradually ebbed away from my limbs. Bond, inconsolable, sat by me, holding my hand.

My eyes popped open. Looking around me like a newborn, I took in a world that everyone believed I had left behind forever.

It took months for me to fully recover physically. I lost almost twenty pounds during my week in a coma, and my brain—miraculously unscathed despite the weeklong bacterial attack—had to work hard to find its bearings again in the physical world.

But the physical recovery was the easy part. There was something else that had to heal as well in the wake of my recovery. I guess you could call it my belief system.

I now believe in angels. Not in some abstract way, but in the same way that I "believe" my car is sitting in my driveway, in the same way that I "believe" that I love my family.

In other words, I don't really "believe" in angels at all. I quite simply know they are real.

During my seven days in a coma, I journeyed to a world above this one: a world indescribably vibrant, vivid, and—most importantly—*real*. When I entered this world, the first thing—the first *person*—that I saw was a beautiful young woman. She had long golden-brown hair, deep-blue eyes, a simple dress of powder blue, indigo, and peach. I realized we were riding on the wing of a butterfly! In fact millions of butterflies surrounded us, vast fluttering waves of them, dipping down and coming back up around us again. It was a river of life and color, moving through the air. As we floated along together above a landscape of staggering beauty—of trees and clouds and waterfalls—she spoke to me in a language beyond words. And what she told me was, in essence, the same thing that the "imaginary" angels had told all those patients of mine over the years. That I was loved. That I was safe. That I would always, always be taken care of.

Today, I'm still a surgeon, and still a man of science. I still believe the brain is a staggeringly sophisticated machine, capable of the most extraordinary feats, both when well and when under attack by illness.

But today, when a patient tells me that he or she has been visited by an angel, I no longer marvel at how clever the brain is in creating such realistic illusions. Angels, I now know, are not illusions at all. I know, because I learned it from my own angel. An angel with blue eyes, whom I met on the wing of a butterfly.

Hope for Mike

Rick Hamlin

THE CALLS CAME WHEN I was at lunch two years ago. I returned to the office to find my voice mail full of urgent messages from California. First from my older sister, Gioia. She was breathless and in a hurry, jumping into her car to drive to the hospital in Long Beach. "Ricky," she said, "we need your help. There's been an accident. Mike was in a plane crash. Right at the airport. He's the only survivor. Five other guys died. He's being rushed to the ER. Please pray. Pray."

My mom was the next to leave a message: "Honey, I don't know if you heard but it's Mike. He was in a plane crash at the airport in Long Beach. I'm heading down there now. He survived. I don't know how he survived but it's very, very serious. We need your prayers. Poor Diane and the girls."

I listened to the messages with a sinking feeling. Mike is my younger sister Diane's husband. He's a big, boisterous guy with bottle-brush blond hair, a loud voice, a louder laugh, and thighs the size of tree trunks. His idea of fun was to ride his bike one hundred miles before breakfast. It was impossible to imagine that anyone so physically fit could be hurt. He was wired and funny and full of energy. When he led grace at family dinner, his voice could be heard all the way down the block.

I felt so helpless. I wanted to be with Diane and her three girls in the hospital waiting room, getting constant updates. I wanted to hug them, talk to them. I wanted to hear it straight from a straight-talking doctor coming out from some swinging ER doors. Was Mike going to live?

I got Gioia on the phone. "They were on a business trip," she said. "They took off from the airport in a small plane. It crashed right after takeoff. The plane was in flames. When they put out the fire, Mike was the only one alive."

He was badly burned. Doctors didn't know yet about brain damage, internal damage. Two of the guys on the plane were not only colleagues but really good friends, Mark and Jeff.

I put down the phone and rocked in my chair, leaning forward, gripping my stomach, hugging it, trying to hold the pain in. There was no prayer for a moment like this except "*Nooooo.*" I couldn't find anything else.

I called my wife, Carol. "I have this feeling that Mike's going to make it," I said, wanting to reach for hope. Grasping at straws. "He's really strong. He's got a strong faith, a strong will to live." Whom was I spinning things for? It didn't take away the pain.

Mike and Diane's friends gathered at the hospital. Many of them were mourning Mark and Jeff. All they could focus on, for now, was the one who survived. He had to make it. Calls, e-mails went back and forth. The doctors worked on Mike all night. They gave him forty pints of blood and ran him through a battery of tests.

There is a litany of medical terms to classify a patient's state, putting into dry, clinical language what is too horrible to describe: "The patient is in critical condition…serious condition…critical but stabilized."

Around midnight my "*nooooo*" changed to a "Please, God, please…" The doctors fed us bits of information. No apparent brain damage. His heart, kidneys, and liver were all right. There was hope for his lungs, even after all that noxious smoke. But second- and third-degree burns covered over a quarter of his body. Once he was stabilized he would have to go to a burn unit for the painful scrubbing of old scarred tissue and grafting of skin.

I felt greedy praying "Please, please" in this terrible disaster. Five good men had been killed, leaving behind wives and children, empty desks, empty beds. "Please, God, can't some good come from this? Can't there be one ray of hope? Don't give up on Mike."

An ambulance rushed Mike to the burn unit. Now a new vigil took over, people sitting by his bed in between his treatments. "He's in a medically induced coma," Diane explained. "That's the only way they can scrub the skin. Otherwise it's too painful."

"Does he look okay?" I asked. A stupid question. But I wanted to know: How is he going to be? Will he still be Mike of the booming voice and the dinner-table prayers? Where was God in all of this? What was going on inside Mike's head?

"He thrashes around," Diane said, "but he does that when he sleeps."

I flew out to see him, bringing my pocket version of the New Testament and Psalms. His head was bandaged, and his right arm and right leg had swaths of gauze that had to be changed every time they scraped off the skin. His eyes were closed, an IV drip in his arm, a feeding tube in his nose. He was a living, breathing miracle. But could he hear me? I touched his free hand. "Hi, Mike," I said. "It's Rick. Here are a few Psalms." I flipped through some pages and read: "For He shall give His angels charge over you, To keep you in all your ways. In their hands they shall bear you up" (Psalm 91:11–12, NKJV). His eyes opened but didn't focus. Then closed again.

For five weeks he stayed that way, in some land between life and death, slowly being healed. Then finally he woke up. He looked into his wife's eyes and asked her what had happened. What accident had he been in?

"I'll tell you when you're ready," Diane said. "Are you ready now?"

He paused, shook his head. Then he had one question. "Was it my fault?"

"No," she said.

Mike was moved to a rehab hospital for physical and occupational therapy. He worked in earnest, walking, stretching, lifting weights, doing puzzles, talking. Daily he was regaining his strength. He was becoming the Mike we remembered, intense, energetic, loud. But there was a sweetness, too, a new appreciation for life. Friends visited him. Friends called and e-mailed. But did he notice that two of his closest friends never came? Was he aware of who was missing?

Two and a half months after the accident Mike was finally ready to come home. Diane sat with him and told him the story, the plane that rose in the sky and fell to the earth. The fire, the quick work of EMTs who saved his life, the deaths of five men. The time in the ER, the burn unit. Tears rolled down his cheeks.

"Do you remember any of this?"

"No," he said. "I don't even remember being in the burn unit. All I remember are two telephone calls from friends. They both said almost the same thing, that they were all right. I wondered why they were telling me that."

"Who?" Diane asked.

"Mark and Jeff. They called."

It made me think of all those prayers we had said, from my first "*nooooo*" to the Psalms I read at his bedside. No, he had no memory of them, but the spiritual world, God's massive support network, had taken charge. Two friends who were now closer to the realm of angels had offered deeper reassurance than any of us could have given. Lost to us, he was borne up by the world beyond.

Mike is back biking again—not exactly one hundred miles before breakfast, but he looks pretty amazing these days. He laughs, he sends me funny e-mails and inspiring messages. He still prays with a voice that can be heard down the block. Last summer he prayed at the dedication of a beachside memorial for Mark. He feels the loss of his friends intensely—he is an intense guy—but he knows he will see them again. That he was saved and they died is still a mystery. But that God has been with them all he has never doubted. Neither have I.

Mom's Vision of Heaven

Crystal McVea

WHEN I WAS TWENTY-FIVE MY mother Marie's long battle with uterine cancer neared its end. She'd bravely fought it off for several years, until she just couldn't fight it anymore. Losing our mother was something none of us children could ever prepare for or even begin to comprehend.

On the very day I turned twenty-five, my mother asked me not to leave her alone. She said she felt strange and scared. I assured her someone would be with her every minute and through the night. The next morning she was unresponsive, and we called for an ambulance. Before it arrived my mother woke up and started weeping inconsolably. She was petrified and filled with sorrow, and she knew her life was ending. I'd never seen her like that, and I tried desperately to console her. I even told her she was only going to the hospital for a checkup.

"Promise me I will come home," my mother said to me. Not knowing what else to say, I made that promise to her. When she arrived in the ER, her oncologist examined her and suggested we have a priest come and give her last rites. My sister Annette and I said a prayer with the priest, while the doctor and a nurse waited just behind us. When the prayer was over, the doctor checked on my mother. He turned to us and said, "She is gone."

Annette and I hugged and cried and tried to find comfort in the belief that Mom was at peace with God. That powerful belief sustains so many people in their darkest hours, and there in the ER it sustained us. Of course, we all yearn to know with certainty that our loved ones are in a better place, but that's not a gift we can ever expect to get. Certainly it is not a gift I ever imagined I'd receive.

But then, just a few minutes after the doctor declared my mother was dead, a nurse in the ER said something unimaginable: "Oh, my God, your mother is alive! Talk to her; talk to her!"

The nurse had seen my mother start to breathe again and open her eyes. We stood there in absolute amazement, and we looked at the oncologist, who was as shocked and baffled as we were. My mother had only occasionally been lucid in the previous weeks, but suddenly she seemed free of pain and in control of her mind and her body. Most remarkably, she had a warm, peaceful smile on her face, something we hadn't seen for the longest time. She was glowing, and she no longer seemed scared. Then she shocked us even more by speaking in a strong, clear voice. And what she said was this:

"I can't believe I've been given the time and the strength to tell you everything I always wanted to say to you but couldn't."

The next six hours were nothing short of a miracle. My mother's vital signs were inexplicably strong, and she was completely calm and in charge. She was moved to a private room, and one by one she spoke to all five of her children and her husband, my father, Nunzie, and gave us loving messages of hope and strength.

"You have always been such a good daughter," my mother told me. "Laurie, I am so proud of you. I love you very much." Can you imagine what it feels like to have your mother tell you she loves you after you thought she was dead? Her doctors simply couldn't explain what happened—only our mother could.

"I saw the other side," she told us. "It is far more beautiful and peaceful than we could ever imagine. I know now in my heart that I will be able to take care of all of you from there."

As much as we all wanted our mother to stay with us, God had a different plan for her. Still, He'd allowed her to come back and share a beautiful message with us—a message each of us would carry in our hearts for the rest of our lives.

Not much later, my mother sat up and told us God was calling her back. She asked us to all hold hands and say the Lord's Prayer and then leave her in peace. A minute or two later, she was in a coma. A few days after that she passed away at the age of forty-seven.

Angels in Heaven

Lorna Byrne

A FEW YEARS AFTER MY husband, Joe, died, I had major surgery lasting six or seven hours. The surgery went fine, and I was put into a postoperative recovery room some distance away from the nurses rather than in one that had constant supervision.

The surgeon told me afterward that they heard the alarms by my bed going off only because the door was inexplicably ajar. I had stopped breathing and the medical team were sure they had lost me.

I found myself on a very wide bright stairway that curved upward. An angel was holding my hand and telling me to hurry. I was very happy and could feel nothing of my human body. I was full of joy; I knew where I was going—to heaven—and I was so happy to be going there. I had no sadness or thoughts of leaving my children behind me.

There were hundreds of souls with me on their way to heaven. With each of them was their guardian angel. In some cases the guardian angel was walking beside them. Others were holding their hand, and in a few cases, the guardian angels—who were enormous—were carrying the souls in their arms with great tenderness, a bit like carrying a baby. The look on each guardian angel's face was one of pure love. Around each soul there were also hundreds of other angels.

I was fascinated, watching the souls on their way to heaven; they were happy, completely at peace; there were no tears, no signs of stress. It was as if in some way, the souls were in a queue to go to heaven. Other souls came down to greet them, and they seemed to talk in a human way with great excitement. I could tell the difference between the souls that hadn't yet reached heaven and those that were greeting them. The souls that had been in heaven for a while were much more radiant, much brighter, and their human appearance was less marked than those of the souls who had just left the earthly world.

The angel beside me was telling me to rush, that we had to hurry. We were going much faster than the other souls, overtaking them, but no one seemed to mind. In fact, some of them called out to me and told me to hurry up. I felt wonderful; I felt perfect. I had left my human body and any pain behind. I was going to where I wanted to be, and I was so happy. I had no fear or anxiety. I had no thoughts at all of anyone left behind—not even my daughter Megan, who was still very young and had already lost a father.

I wasn't allowed to stop and ask questions. I didn't know why I had to move so fast, but it seemed in some way to be natural. The journey seemed to go on for ages, but in other ways it was a very short journey. Time is different in heaven.

When I got to wherever I was meant to be in heaven, I was suddenly alone, not an angel in sight, although I know my guardian angel was still there. It was as if there was beautiful sand under my bare feet, and I could feel the smooth, silky, warm sand between my toes. The sand was in small hills, and I could see a beautiful tree in the distance on top of one of the hills. The tree was big, covered in leaves, and looked perfect in every way.

I hadn't a care in the world. It was like being a little child again. I went and sat down under the tree for a little while and then started playing at rolling down the hill. After a short while, I heard a voice and knew immediately it was God's.

"Lorna, you must go back," the voice boomed. This was my second near-death experience. The first time, I had begged to be allowed to stay in heaven. This time

I didn't protest, as I knew I wouldn't be listened to anyway. An angel took me by the hand—I have no idea which angel it was—and brought me back. I have no memory of coming back into my body.

Some weeks later, the surgeon told me that I had been gone for ten minutes, and they hadn't been sure whether they could revive me or not. Some days after the operation, I became conscious in intensive care. The surgeon expected me to have brain damage, and was surprised that there were no signs of it.

I know that one of the reasons I have been given these experiences is so that I can share them with all of you. So that I can help you to understand that there is nothing to fear in death.

Eternity's Door

Mary C. Neal, MD

MY HUSBAND, BILL, AND I had gone to Chile for a white-water kayaking vacation. Bill, like me, is an orthopedic surgeon and we share a practice, along with a love of outdoor adventure. We had paddled on some of the roughest rivers in the United States, and this was a chance to try our stuff on the wild, untamed waters of the Chilean Andes. We left our four young children at home with our longtime babysitter and traveled to one of the remotest corners of the globe.

Snow-fed rivers tumbled down volcanic slopes, with challenging ten- and twenty-foot drops, perfect for us. Our guides were our good friends, Tom and Debbi Long, along with their sons. They'd been hosting white-water trips to Chile for years and knew exactly where to go and what we'd face. Still, that morning, I had an uneasy feeling. Maybe it was because Bill was going to take the day off—he had some back pain that was bothering him. (You'd think that with both of us in the business we could avoid that!) Or maybe it was because a new, less-experienced group of boaters was joining us that day. I just had this strange, shadowy feeling.

"Sure I can't convince you?" I asked Bill one last time. "I can fix whatever's ailing you."

Bill chuckled. "I'll take the truck and meet you at the takeout," he said. "I'll find a nice place to read and enjoy the scenery." The views of thick subtropical forests and snow-covered peaks were breathtaking. Civilization was far away. I almost envied him his peace and quiet.

"Okay," I said. "Give me your paddling jacket." His was bright red, unlike my drab one. At least he could spot me easily from shore, and I'd have a part of him with me.

He drove us to the put-in. I slipped on his jacket and kissed him good-bye. Then I joined the rest of the group and we stepped into our boats. "We'll stop before we hit our first big drop," Tom said. I put my feet against the foot braces and tightened the spray skirt around my waist. It would keep water out of the boat and my lower half dry. If a kayaker gets into trouble she can pull the loop, or "pull the chute" as we say, to release the spray skirt and escape the boat quickly.

Out of the corner of my eye I watched the new kayakers. One in particular wasn't so sure of herself. I steered around her. We paddled downriver, stopping at the eddy above the falls. There was a narrow channel to the right and a larger main channel to the left. "We'll take the smaller channel," Tom called over the water's roar. "It's more predictable."

Good move, I thought, remembering the inexperienced kayaker. The left channel looked pretty hairy.

The first boater paddled down the channel on the right. I followed. The current moved swiftly. We headed forward. Suddenly her boat turned at an angle. She was being whipped sideways by the current. Then her boat got lodged between two boulders. She jumped out and waded to shore, leaving her kayak on the rocks.

I'm going to have to go left. There was no stopping my momentum. I took a deep breath and plunged fifteen, twenty feet down the falls. My boat dove straight down. The force of the water was crushing. It ripped the paddle from my hands. I smashed into some submerged rocks. My crazy dive stopped. Still upright, I was pinned. Trapped underwater. I couldn't paddle. Couldn't move. The waterfall was so strong it held me down. My arms flopped in the vicious current. No one would ever see me in the turbulence, even with Bill's blazing red jacket.

Pull the chute! I screamed silently. I grasped for the loop. Couldn't reach it. The force against my arms was too strong. I pushed against the foot braces. Nothing. I tried to jiggle the boat. I desperately raised my head. Fresh air was only a couple of feet above me but I couldn't reach it. It was no use. I was stuck. My kayak, my coffin. *You're not in control,* I told myself. *Just let go.*

I thought of Bill and our four kids, our family, our orthopedic practice. *God,* I prayed, *I know You love me and have a plan for me. Thy will be done.*

It was precisely at that instant something shifted in me, like a spiritual jolt. A great calm took me. It was like being a baby rocked and caressed in a mother's arms. I had this absolutely certain sense that everything would be okay, no matter what happened. I was overwhelmed by this peace. It completely transcended my panic and dread. I felt myself stop struggling. What about Bill and the children? Would they be all right? Could they survive without me? But that profound reassurance eased all my doubts. "Okay, God," I said. "Hurry up."

At once the wild current grabbed me, jerking me out of my kayak. My knees folded back under me. I was dragged and battered by the river. I observed it clinically, dispassionately, as though I was my own patient: "Your knee bones just broke... You just tore your ligaments..."

And then the strangest thing yet—with something I can only describe as a *pop* my soul separated from my body.

I shot above the river into another realm. Fifteen or twenty human spirits rushed forward to welcome me. We hugged and danced. I could not identify them but I knew that I knew them, even with their outlines blurred. They were sent by God to guide me.

We began to glide along a path. We were going home. My eternal home. My companions could barely contain their joy. Joy at the instant of death. A feeling of absolute love pierced me, a feeling greater and so different from anything I'd ever known. We were bathed in a light brighter than I had ever seen. I turned and looked down. Below me I glimpsed my body on the riverbank, the shell of an old friend.

Tom and his sons were beside my body. "Breathe, Mary, breathe!" they screamed, giving me CPR. I loved them and didn't want them to be sad. *You could go back for just one breath,* I thought. At that, I flew down and took a breath, then instantly went back to my companions.

We traveled a path that led to a great hall, larger and more beautiful than anything I could conceive of, with an immense dome and a central arch built with shimmering gold blocks. I felt my soul gravitate toward the entrance, absorbed by the ever-present radiance. Heaven. Irresistible paradise. Eternal home. I was flooded with an intense longing to be reunited with God.

Still Tom and his sons kept beckoning. Each time they begged me to take a breath I felt obligated to return quickly to my body and take another breath before continuing my journey. I grew impatient. *I need to keep traveling. Let me go.*

I understood everything my spiritual companions told me, even though they didn't speak. All our thoughts simply merged. We were right at the archway with the golden bricks. Suddenly they turned to me. "Not yet," they said. "It's not your time to enter. You have more to do on earth." Sorrow filled me, as powerful as the great joy had been. I knew I had to go back, back to life. Yet I knew I would also return. Someday. Just not now.

I opened my eyes to see the faces of the Longs staring at me. They were amazed to see me conscious. I'd been "dead" for over eleven minutes. I couldn't move my legs and assumed I'd broken my back.

The trip up the hillside and my reunion with Bill was filled with one miracle after another: like the mysterious ambulance that appeared out of nowhere in this remote wilderness and the helpers who assisted us, then disappeared. Our trip back to the States was an incredible journey, an odyssey. There, I recovered slowly from my injuries (fortunately I diagnosed myself wrong; I did not break my back, thank God). But it's taken even more time to absorb my experience.

In the thirteen years since, I have seen how my work as a mom, a wife, and a doctor has not been over. My most important job is to tell this story. Perhaps it was entrusted to me because I am a doctor and I think in terms of facts and objective knowledge. But there is another world to which we're called and it is the most true and beautiful we will ever experience. Our eternal home awaits us.

Angel Wings

Brenda Boswell

THIS PRECIOUS STORY HAS BEEN shared only in my family through the years, but for the first time it seemed right to tell others.

My mother, Irene, was Irish/Native Indian, born in Oklahoma. She was sweet, gentle, and infinitely courageous. When this event happened, Momma told us she was in her young twenties, and she lived in a small southern Oklahoma town apartment in the 1940s. She was pregnant with my older brother, John. My daddy was off serving his country as a Navy code breaker. It was summer, and the Oklahoma heat could be deadly. There was no air-conditioning in those days so all windows and doors in the apartment were open to catch a breeze.

This was the first child for my parents, and my momma was understandably scared of this new and overwhelming experience. The good thing was family was always nearby to offer support…and so it was on the fateful day. Momma was having a tough day. She felt something was wrong. She was in great pain and my brother, John, wasn't due for several weeks. The hometown doctor was called and he came right away to their apartment. He delivered a stillborn baby boy. My momma was devastated. Daddy was far away at war, and a great sense of grief and loss overwhelmed her.

I have to tell you our family has deep spiritual roots … rich in Irish and Native Indian traditions. My momma had it in spades. This day she turned to our precious Lord for comfort and help. What happened next, as Momma told us, was that she struggled to go into the kitchen within an hour of losing the baby and there on the kitchen curtains was an imprint of baby angel wings. She looked several times to be certain she was not having a dream episode. No, it was true. Clear wing markings indicated an angel baby had departed from their home. Momma cried as she told this part of the story. They were tears of recognition, she said, because she knew without doubt in seeing the images on the curtain that her beloved baby boy, John, was in heaven.

Even today, sixty years later, I am quite in awe of God's graciousness and merciful comfort given to my mother and to little angel boy, John.

The Coventry Game

Ben Hall as told to Laraine Anne Barker

"CAMILLA, JANINE, LISTEN TO ME!" I yelled above the *boom! boom!* of the stereo.

But my sisters wouldn't. I could tell by their refusal to look at me they'd sent me to Coventry again. (To "send someone to Coventry" is a British idiom meaning to banish or ostracize a person, to refuse to talk to them or pretend they don't exist.) They were masters at pretending you weren't there. They'd had enough practice. I was always being sent to Coventry—mostly for lying. Camilla said nobody twisted the truth as much as I did. All I can say is, she should listen to herself!

Only this time I wasn't lying. Our brother, Damon, really had crashed the car. He'd scoffed at how easy driving was. After all, he argued, he'd watched Dad often enough and was starting lessons the next day. But he lost control the moment he turned the car onto the road. It rolled over and over down a steep bank into one of our fields. And Damon was hurt badly. He'd asked me to run for help. My sisters, I'd reckoned, should know what to do. After all, they were older than me. Only I hadn't bargained on them playing that hateful, childish game when I'd done nothing to deserve it. And they'd never played it as well as they were now.

Camilla pressed the CD player's Stop button. "I'm sick of that. It's not as good as their first. Where's your new Oasis?"

Maybe they hadn't heard above the blaring music. I yelled again, begging them to listen. My voice was shatteringly loud in the brief silence. My throat started to choke up. *I mustn't cry,* I commanded myself. *That's what they want.*

Janine calmly handed her CD to Camilla, who placed it onto the turntable and set it playing. If anything it seemed noisier than the first one.

I wanted to shake those two silly girls. No—batter them with my fists! But that would start a fight. I'd long learned it was cowardly for a boy to hit a girl, even one bigger than himself.

It was no good. I was going to have to find Mum or Dad. And they could be anywhere on the farm.

"You two are beastly! If Damon dies, it'll be *your* fault!" I yelled into Camilla's ear, stamping my feet in frustrated fury.

She still took no notice. Her acting was superb. Fighting tears, I slammed out of the house.

Only later I wondered why I hadn't phoned for an ambulance. But I wasn't thinking clearly. I couldn't even *see* clearly—although that was probably because of tears.

Now where were my parents likely to be? I peered at my watch, blinking to bring it into focus. Four o'clock. That meant Dad would be milking. And Mum? Oh yes. Ebony, her favorite mare, was about to have her first foal, and the vet warned there might be problems. Mum was checking on Ebony. Well, Mum was a nurse before she married Dad and became a farmer. Besides, the stables were closer than the milking shed.

I tore across the garden. At the other end of the lawn, Mum's twenty-four white doves scattered in a startled flurry of soft wings. They usually flew toward me the moment they saw me and were now looked upon as mine. But I had no time to ponder the reason for their odd behavior.

I reached the stables to find the foal born and Mum trying to clean herself up. She looked up, startled, when I yelled, "Mum! Mum! Damon's crashed the car! He's hurt! Come quickly!"

She squinted at me as though her eyes couldn't focus. "Speak slowly, Ben. You're babbling again."

I skidded to a halt and repeated what I'd said, this time giving more detail to stop the endless questions I knew would follow.

She looked shocked but otherwise took it in the calm manner that I suppose she'd learned from her medical training. "Have you rung for an ambulance?"

I shook my head. I was beyond words now. She grabbed the wall phone and grimly dialed in the emergency number. Then I had to wait while she dialed again and spoke to a paramedic who lived locally. She put the phone back and strode toward me, blinking as well as squinting. "I can't see you properly. You look all blurred. I must be starting a migraine."

How could she worry about something as trifling as a headache with Damon in danger?

"Hurry!" I yelled as I turned and ran. But she'd already broken into a run. Fortunately she asked no more questions.

I could hear Damon moaning before we reached the car. *That's good,* I thought in relief. (I'd heard on TV that the noisy victims in an accident were the least hurt.) *And thank goodness the car landed on its wheels.*

It had come to rest with the passenger side facing us. I was racing past the mangled hood to the driver's side when Mum's shriek brought me up sharp.

"*Be-en!*"

"Yeah?" I rushed back in alarm.

But she didn't answer, just yanked at the front passenger door handle. She had to put all her weight into it before the door gave with a sickening crunch. And I saw there was someone in the seat. My surroundings whirled around me.

I was staring at myself!

I won't describe what I looked like—except that, under all the blood, my face was so white I knew I was dead. *So this me looking on must be a spirit,* I thought in bewilderment. *That's why I was able to move so fast.* For I now remembered how

I'd passed through everything, even spiny barberry hedges. I hadn't realized it at the time. And that was why I'd spooked my doves.

Then I couldn't see anything. The car, Mum, my own dead face, all darkened and blurred. The sky turned black. But only for a moment. A blinding light zapped out of it. I squinted into it. It settled into a warm, soothing glow, surrounded by a whirling darkness like a huge funnel. Something moved within the light at the funnel's center. For a moment I couldn't make out what it was. I strained to see— for some reason it seemed important that I should know what was at the heart of the light. After some effort I did: two human-like creatures clad in white with huge, white wings framing their shining faces.

Angels! And they were beckoning to me. As they did so, something fluttered around their heads, white and looking as soft as their wings.

Doves—symbols of peace and happiness.

We have a flock of doves in our garden, I told the angels.

The doves—lovely, graceful creatures—came spiraling down the tunnel. I could hear the slow *whit whit whit* of their wings—a magical sound. Against the black of the whirling tunnel they seemed to have a light of their own. And they were coming for me. They wanted to take me to their world, to share the wonder of winged flight with me. That black whirling tunnel that I had to go through first wouldn't be frightening at all with them all around me. Eagerly I stretched out my arms to them.

Their soft feathers cushioned me and started lifting me just as I felt something else: pain in my chest as though something pressed against it.

"No, Ben, no! You can't die! No! No! Come back! I won't let you die." It was my mother's voice.

"Let me go!" I screamed. "I want to fly with the doves and be an angel." But somehow I knew the words were only in my mind. And what about Damon?

If Mum was going to waste time trying to bring me back to life, how could she look after him? After all, I'd walked away from the crash....

But I didn't, I reminded myself numbly. *I'm dead. And I can't stay with Mum and go with the doves and the angels as well.*

Something pressed my fingers. A hand—a trembling hand. I couldn't see the angels or the doves anymore. I couldn't even see the light. There was only darkness. And pain, unbearable pain.

"Come on, Ben, come on! You can make it! I'm sorry I forgot to remind you to put your seat belt on." That was Damon's voice, hoarse with threatening tears. So he was going to be all right. And I wasn't ready to die yet either.

"I'm coming, Mum! I'm coming!" I cried, striving with all my might to get out of the whirling darkness that now surrounded me.

They said I opened my eyes at Damon's words. They said I was conscious when the paramedics put the oxygen mask over my face. Only I don't remember. My first and clearest memory is opening my eyes in the hospital to find my sisters staring anxiously down at me.

"You're going to be all right. The doctors say you'll make a full recovery," Camilla assured me. "And Damon's coming home today."

Later, when I told them how they had ignored my ghostly pleas (I even repeated their own words to prove I'd been there), their eyes widened in wonder.

"We're sorry for ignoring you," Janine said, tears choking her voice. "Only we didn't hear you—honestly. It's just as well Mum did, even if she couldn't see you properly. And we'll never *ever* send you to Coventry again."

Well, that was a long time ago. My sisters are young women now, and they kept their word.

Comforted by My Angels
Crystal McVea

DURING A HOSPITAL STAY, I left my body for nine minutes and went to heaven. I was instantly aware of two beings in front of me who were to my left, and I knew right away they were angels.

But they weren't just any angels—they were *my* angels.

I recognized them immediately. There was so much brightness coming off them that I couldn't make out any features. But they weren't shapeless blobs; they definitely had a form, which was roughly that of a human body: long and slender. The being on the right appeared a bit bigger than the one on the left. They didn't move or hover or anything—they were just there.

And what I instantly felt for them was love.

A great, sweeping love for my angels overwhelmed me. It was like they were the best friends I could ever have, though the word *friend* doesn't come close to describing them. The angels were my protectors, my teachers, my mentors, my heroes, my strength, my spirit, my heart, everything, all rolled into one. I felt like they had been a part of my existence and my journey forever—as if they had been by my side for every tear I ever cried, every decision I had ever made, every day I ever felt lonely, not only on Earth but through all eternity. I felt so unbelievably safe and free in their presence, so happy and fulfilled. I understood why they were there—to greet me upon my arrival and guide me back home. They were the best welcoming committee you could ask for.

What's more, I realized there was instant and complete communication between us. What do I mean by that? Imagine a button you can press; as soon as you press it, you know everything there is to know about someone, and they know everything about you. Or a password that, if you let me use it, gives me instant access to everything you've ever said or thought or felt or written or believed in your life: past, present, and future. Instantly, I would have a more complete understanding of you than is possible on Earth. Well, that is what this was like—a sensation that everything we were, everything that mattered, was passing freely between my angels and me, strengthening our profound connection and an eternal bond. There was no room whatsoever for secrets or shame or misunderstanding or anything negative.

There was just this wonderful, beautiful, nourishing sense of *knowing*.

I wish I could say I recognized them as people I previously knew on Earth, but I didn't. Many who have died describe seeing a favorite relative waiting for them in the beyond. They talk about the amazing joy of such a heavenly reunion. I would love to have been reunited with my precious grandma Ernie, but I wasn't. I'm not saying that doesn't happen; it just wasn't part of my experience. Still, meeting my angels left me overflowing with joy. They never left my side, and I knew they never would.

CHAPTER 5

Touched by an Angel

The Handsome Stranger

Joan Wester Anderson

HAROLD AND BEULAH BASSLER, AN elderly couple from Martinsburg, Pennsylvania, were enjoying their usual after-church Sunday drive. They were on a small country road, admiring the scenery, when suddenly a large car approached. The driver (whom they later discovered was drunk) was aiming right for them. Harold swerved, but there was nowhere for their car to go except off the road. It bounced down an embankment and toppled into a gushing stream. Harold and Beulah both shouted for help.

Fortunately, within minutes, many people in the area ran to assist them. It was a small town, and just about everyone knew everyone else. As some of the men hung on to the car, and others grabbed the Basslers to keep them from being pulled away by the current, everyone saw a handsome blue-eyed stranger drive up and stop. "Here, let me help. They're going to be cold!" he said, grabbing two brand-new sleeping bags from inside his spotless automobile. As the neighbors pulled Harold and Beulah out of the water, they tore off their outer clothes and laid each one inside a sleeping bag. When the ambulance arrived, the attendants left the couple in the warm bags while they drove them to Nason Hospital in Roaring Springs, Pennsylvania.

Excitement over, everyone now looked around for the handsome stranger. But he was nowhere to be found. How could someone have driven off without anyone noticing? And why had he arrived on a little-traveled road—with those comfortable sleeping bags—at just the right time?

Due to the warm bags preventing hypothermia, the Basslers survived their ordeal, and they had several happy years together afterward. No one ever saw the stranger again. But there was one more peculiar postscript: Not only did the stranger disappear, the sleeping bags did too. Uncle Weldon Bassler attempted to retrieve them from the hospital, to have them cleaned and possibly returned to the mystery man. But he was greeted with blank looks from the emergency room staff.

"Sleeping bags?" more than one replied. "I don't recall seeing them at all."

Now I Remember!

William T. Porter

WE WERE STANDING IN MY parents' front yard saying good-bye when we heard her scream—it was our little daughter, two-and-a-half.

Rushing to the backyard, we found Helen standing in the center of the flagstone sidewalk, crying and dripping wet. It was apparent that she had fallen into my parents' small but deep fish pond. Thank God she was safe!

Then, as my wife rushed over to pick Helen up, it hit me. I couldn't see any wet footprints anywhere around the pond, yet our baby was standing a good twenty feet away from the water. The only water was the puddle where she stood dripping. And there was no way a toddler could have climbed out of the pool by herself—it was six or seven feet in diameter and about four feet deep.

As Helen grew up, we often puzzled over those strange circumstances. She herself had no memory of the event; she was, however, haunted by an intense fear of water.

Many years later, when Helen and her soldier-husband were living in San Antonio, she began to work through that fear with the help of an army chaplain, Pastor Claude Ingram. After spiritual counseling and prayer sessions, he asked her to go back in memory and relive the frightening fish-pond experience. She put herself in the scene again and began describing the pond and the fish in detail. She cried out as she relived the moment of falling into the water. Then suddenly Helen gasped. "Now I remember!" she said. "He grabbed me by the shoulders and lifted me out!"

"Who did?" asked Pastor Ingram.

"Someone in white," she answered. "Someone pulled me out, then left."

A Still, Small Voice

Lyn McConchie

WHEN I WAS TEN I started at a new school. On my first day there I met a girl named Karen. We clicked at once, maybe because we were complete opposites in many ways. While we were of similar height, she had brown hair and blue eyes while my hair was black and my eyes brown. I was a skinny, scrawny kid and Karen was sturdier and moved deliberately, where I moved as if I was always in a hurry. I played almost every sport there was, while she roller-skated and that was it. She was an only child with loving parents, while I was the foster child of guardians who ill-treated me constantly.

Over the years we remained loyal friends. We both married, attended each other's weddings, and worked in government employment. Neither marriage was wonderful, but she stayed in hers. "I made my vows to God," she told me, "no matter what." I divorced and felt under no obligation to remain with a dishonest man. Yet despite these different attitudes, Karen and I stayed friends.

Friends through my having cancer once and her having it twice. Friends through my living all over the country and her staying right in the town where she was born. Friends despite her being a devout Christian and me being somewhat of a nonreligious type. Friends through the two major accidents I had that left me crippled, needing to use a crutch to get about. No longer able to work in normal employment, I began to write, and Karen obtained a proofreader's qualification and proofread my books for me.

Then her husband died and she was bereft. Worse still, she became unwell, and I went to stay with her in another city while she had medical tests. It was to me she turned then when the verdict was given. Ovarian cancer, and she had about a year. I visited as often as I could. We talked about old times at school as we laughed at the incidents remembered from then—I could always make her laugh. And before she went into a hospice for the last time, I wrote her a letter to say how much she'd always meant to me. (It was found in her possession after her death with the paragraph in which I'd told her of that, highlighted.)

I saw her only a few days before she died quietly in her sleep, and she thanked me for always having been there for her. I said that was what friends were for and made her laugh with a silly joke. Then she was gone. For so long it had been Lyn and Karen, now it was Lyn and...Lyn and...We'd been friends for fifty-three years and I missed her. I still do.

Of course, life went on. That following winter we had horrific weather. On my small farm, which is at some 1,600 feet, the storm winds were brutal. They struck again one afternoon, gusting at around eighty-one miles per hour. I was alone in the kitchen when I heard a rending sound: without thinking I went out of the door and stood listening to the tearing noises. I couldn't see anything and to see better, I went out to step past the big concrete water tank a few feet from the door. Right then I felt a hand catch at my arm and heard: "LYN. STOP!" It was a voice I'd known for fifty-three years.

Involuntarily I stopped. Just then there was a long, metallic ripping shriek and a whirling sheet of roofing iron came slashing overhead past the tank. I froze, another passed, and a third. I spun on my heel, diving for the door and safety as more and more of the big covered-sheep-yards' roof was torn apart and carried past me on the gale. Had I been hit by any of those whirling sheets of iron I'd have died or been badly injured. When the storm passed, friends helped me demolish what was left of the yards, and recover the iron, several sheets of which had left deep gashes in the trunks of the trees that had stopped them from going still farther.

And, for the first time in many years, I prayed. For a friend I'd loved, and in thanks that somehow she'd been there for me. And I knew that God sent her as my protector in that storm. Our love and friendship survive. I know that one day I'll see my friend again. I know I don't walk alone. I know that God and His angels don't sleep. They keep a watchful eye on all of my comings and goings, and not just in storms.

All Day, All Night

Pat Larimore

I'M A REGISTERED NURSE, AND I take care of patients in their homes once they've been released from the hospital. A few days after Christmas I was finishing a shift when my babysitter called. "Pat, I don't know what to do," she cried. "Amber woke up with her cheek all swollen, and her temperature's more than a hundred and four!"

"I'm on my way," I said. My nine-month-old daughter had just started teething. The fever and swelling sounded like an infection. Probably nothing to worry about, but I dialed the pediatrician just to make sure.

As soon as I described Amber's symptoms, her doctor said, "Meet me at the hospital. Right away."

I raced home, trying not to panic. Amber lay in her crib, glassy-eyed, looking as if she had a golf ball in her cheek. "Grab her diaper bag. We've got to hurry," I told the babysitter as I scooped my daughter into my arms.

We were met at the hospital by the pediatrician, who whisked Amber into an exam room. My nurse's training to remain composed and objective in a crisis crumbled. I felt frightened, helpless, like any mother with a dangerously sick child. I prayed and prayed and prayed.

Finally, there was a diagnosis: A nasty virus had entered my daughter's bloodstream through the opening in her gums where her teeth were coming in. She couldn't be released until her temperature came down.

In the days that followed, my husband, my mother, and I took turns sitting with Amber. At night I slept on a cot next to her crib. "*Shh*, you'll be all right, honey," I said softly when she cried, comforting her till she was calm again. How I wished someone could do the same for me!

By New Year's Eve, I was exhausted. That evening, still feverish, Amber finally dozed off, and I collapsed on the cot. Well after midnight I was awakened—by what, I wasn't sure. I didn't hear my baby crying. I checked the crib.

That's when I saw her sitting on the other side—an elderly woman in a blue dress and glasses, rocking a peacefully sleeping Amber in her arms. *One of the volunteers on the ward*, I thought groggily. *Amber's okay.*

The woman smiled and gestured at me to go back to sleep. Whatever it was about her that soothed my daughter, it worked on me too. I drifted off again easily.

The next morning I got up feeling rested and refreshed. Reflexively I put my hand on Amber's forehead. It was cool! A nurse took her temperature and confirmed the fever had broken.

"Do you know the name of that elderly volunteer who was here around midnight?" I asked. "I want to thank her for watching Amber."

The nurse looked at me quizzically. "We don't have any volunteers in the middle of the night."

But God does. All day and all night.

Jailhouse Rock

Josh Gilbert as told to Morna Gilbert

THE THIN BUNK SMELLED PUTRID. My head lay on the limp makeshift pillow as I stared at the cold gray wall. *How did I get here? Was I really that stupid?* I wanted to scream but I couldn't. I wanted to run but the three cement walls and row of vertical steel bars kept me caged like an animal. I put my hands over my ears to try to keep out the sounds of yelling, cursing, snoring, ranting, banging, when abruptly the door to my cell opened as a guard pushed an old gray-haired man into my new home.

This man—whose name I soon learned was Clarence—slowly looked at his surroundings, shuffled his weary feet to his bunk, sat, and laid his creaky body down with a grunt. He stared at his wall, ignoring me completely. I heard him mutter, "Stupid kid—why do I have to be with a stupid kid?"

Hours passed. Our cell had an awkward silence surrounded by the chaotic clanging of doors and loud voices of disgruntled men. I hated this. My gut was wrenched with the sick feeling of abandonment and guilt. As I lay there thinking of my wife and my two little girls, I found myself quietly weeping. *Was what I did this bad?*

"Yes, Josh, it was," said the voice in my head. "You are reaping what you sowed."

But, God, I was joking! I wasn't serious!

"Yes, you were."

Do You still love me, Lord?

"I discipline those I love. I am proving My love for you right now."

This doesn't feel like love. This feels like hell. Get me out of here! I only know I felt more alone than I had ever been in my entire life. The sobbing came freely. My gut exploded into a flood of tears that could not be contained. My body quivered in anguish. *I'm twenty years old. I have my life ahead of me. What have I done?* My head screamed as I cried uncontrollably now. *It would be easier to die than to endure this pain.*

"Ya ever heard of Elvis, kid?"

It took me a minute, but I gained a bit of composure, wiped my nose on my sleeve, and turned my head to see Clarence sitting on his bunk. *Gosh, he's old....*

"I asked you—ever heard of Elvis?" His eyes twinkled—just a touch.

"Yeah—he's my grandma's favorite."

"Can ya sing?"

"What?"

"Can ya sing? Sometimes it helps to sing."

"Well...a little...I guess."

What happened over the next few moments would have been enough to turn the real Elvis over in his grave—I'm sure of it.

Clarence sat on his bunk pretending he was holding a guitar—strumming away—he began to sing like there was no tomorrow and like he was the real king of rock.

"The warden threw a party in the county jail...the prison band was there and they began to wail...let's rock, everybody, let's rock...dancin' to the jailhouse rock."

"Come on, kid. Sing it with me!"

I mustered up some strength to forget the reality of where I was and chimed along. By the time we were done we were both laughing.

Clarence looked me in the eyes and said, "Kid, no matter what happens...sing. And then smile. You gotta good smile and this ol' world just needs to smile more."

Honestly, I just couldn't see myself ever really wanting to sing in this place. It's too dark. It's depressing. It's demeaning. It's beyond pain-filled. *Sing? How?*

When I awoke the next morning Clarence was nowhere to be found. No inmate or guard had heard of him.

Since this story was published, I've served over two-thirds of my prison sentence. Leading the worship service five times a week has been no small part of what's kept me alive...and happy. My number-one ministry tool, that helps others like me come to know and love God? My smile.

Change of Heart

Bella Gatti

IT WAS A COLD AND drizzling night in town. I pulled up my hood on my red jacket and muttered to myself as I walked alone, splashing in the puddles that gathered on the uneven sidewalks. I wasn't in any hurry to go home.

Before dinner my family had gotten into a funk. We began arguing and blaming, I was heated and angry, and tears sent me outside to clear my head and cool down.

As I neared the bus stop, I noticed a woman alone waiting. She stopped me to ask if I knew when the next bus would come. I looked at the tiny print on the schedule but told her I couldn't see it. She said, "You can use my glasses," which I did. I read the times and told her it ought to be there within a few minutes.

She held my hand and thanked me for being so kind. All of that took barely a minute or two, then I turned away. I didn't take more than a dozen steps when I suddenly felt light and free from all that had sent me out into the rain.

The woman's bus rattled by me. I turned, wanting to catch another glimpse of the person who had changed my mood with barely a conversation and hardly a touch. But the bus didn't stop and continued on, for no one was waiting there.

When I got back home, I held the hands of my husband and daughter, and one at a time we said, "I love you, I am sorry, please forgive me, thank you." We cried, but we loved again. *Where did that woman in the rain come from?*

Gifts from Heaven

Kelly Smith

WHAT BIRDS HAVE WHITE FEATHERS? Doves, seagulls, even swans. It's not so rare to find a white feather when you're outside. But when these feathers appear out of nowhere and you're indoors and they all look the same...Could they be feathers from angel wings? Little gifts from heaven to remind us that this life is not the only life? That Someone is watching over us? That's what I've come to think.

This is what happened.

The news was heart-wrenching. My dad phoned early one Saturday morning telling me that my older brother, Neil, was dead. His body had been found near a main road; no one knew what had happened. Only later would we learn that he had been killed in a hit-and-run accident. I don't know how I found a flight from New York, where I was in my last year of college, to my hometown of Dundee, Scotland, on that same day, but I did. And I booked it with no return date. I knew I would be staying awhile—I needed to be with my mom, dad, and brother, as well as with my brother's close group of friends, and take in this shock together.

Twenty-four hours later, my brother's best friend, Mark, and I walked along the narrow stone streets of Dundee. It was a damp and cold October night. With his face half-hidden by his sweatshirt hood, Mark told me about the night Neil died. They had been at the pub with other officers in the Scottish Police Services Authority, where Neil worked. Mark left about midnight; Neil stayed and then decided to walk to Mark's house—a decision that had led to his death. His voice cracked as Mark said, "The last thing I said to Neil was that I'd leave the key under the plant pot at the door." We stood for a moment in silence. And then a white feather fell on his hood. It seemed natural to say, "The angels are telling you it's okay, it's not your fault."

* * *

MARK AND HIS WIFE, LEE, were expecting their first child. The sudden shock, meetings with detectives as they were trying to determine cause of Neil's death, and grief were taking their toll. Lee's doctor recommended bed rest for the rest of the pregnancy. But Mark and Lee came to the funeral. When it was over, and we were walking out of the church, Lee came to me. "This fell on my belly during the service," she said softly, handing me a white feather. It was the same size and the same color as the first feather. And it appeared indoors! *Angels are telling us the baby is going to be okay,* is what ran through my mind.

* * *

A MONTH PASSED AND I needed to return to college. My mom and dad drove me to the airport and we said a tearful good-bye. It was November, and I had plans to come back to Scotland for Christmas. When I arrived in New York, I got a call from Mom. "Kelly, when we got back to the house, we found another feather. A big white feather was lying in the hallway, in front of the picture of you and Neil when he came to visit you in New York."

* * *

MOM WAS DIAGNOSED WITH BREAST cancer that December, just weeks after my brother died. I was back in New York, feeling like the world was turning upside down. My dad was devastated; his son was dead and now this. Unlike the rest of us, he took no comfort from the feathers. Wearily, he got into the car one morning after dropping my mom off at her first chemo appointment. On the passenger seat where my mother had just been sitting moments before was a white feather.

* * *

I WAS DRIVING IN PENNSYLVANIA a few months later, heading to visit a friend. It was snowing heavily, and my small car kept losing traction going up the mountains, and sliding going down. I wiped my sweaty hands on my jeans, gripping the wheel tightly. Just then, I felt someone in the car with me. Calmly, I continued down the mountain. At the bottom, I took a deep breath and relaxed. That's when I noticed there was a white feather on my lap.

* * *

MY MOM KEEPS ALL OF these feathers in a memory box with other things of Neil's. When I go back home to Scotland, I like to go through this box. I hold the feathers together in a bouquet and, wondering and remembering, feel happy and safe. I'm reminded of Psalm 91:4 (NIV), which reads: "He will cover you with his feathers, and under his wings you will find refuge; his faithfulness will be your shield and rampart."

Little Blond Boy

Louise Ringhee

MY HUSBAND, JAMES, WAS A drinker. We'd been married fifteen years, and every day he wasn't working he hit the bars as soon as they opened. Beer after beer washed down shot after shot of whiskey. Then he'd come home and scream at me, "You're nothing!"

That particular summer afternoon, James stumbled in and snarled, "Gimme some money." I didn't have any. I was terrified he'd start hitting me. Again.

Abruptly, James staggered toward me and knocked me over. Then he went out, slamming the screen door behind him. I heard his truck squeal out of our driveway while I lay on the floor, sobbing. *I can't go on like this, Lord.*

After picking myself up and snatching my keys, I left the house. *For the last time*, I thought as I got into my Plymouth Duster. In my mind, one of us had to die for this situation to end. And I was going to be the one.

I headed toward the bridge, intent upon driving my car off it. I had that utter sense of clarity that overwhelming despair sometimes brings. *It's the only way,* I thought. As I passed by the community pool, I saw a little blond boy in swim trunks standing on the corner, crying and rubbing his eyes with his fists. Must have lost his mommy.

Pulling over to the curb, I called out the window, "Are you okay, honey?" He shook his head. "My daddy forgot to pick me up." My heart went out to the little towhead. He must have felt so abandoned. "Come on, I'll take you home," I offered. He looked at me, then opened the car door and climbed in.

"Where do you live?" I asked. "Just show me where to go."

He told me to turn right at the next corner and directed me to the outskirts of town. Tidy rows of houses greeted us. It was a neighborhood I'd never been in before. These developments were springing up everywhere. He pointed at a new ranch house. "That's it!" he cried. I stopped. "Here you are, sweetie," I said. "Thanks," he called as he rushed into the house. In the driveway there was a man working under the hood of a car.

"I brought your boy home," I hollered, then drove on.

I passed the bridge on the way back to town. But my desire to kill myself had been replaced with a sense of hope and renewed faith. Amazingly, my attitude felt stronger than it had in years.

I joined a spousal support group and gained an understanding of what it means to be in an abusive marriage. It took time, work, and prayer, but eventually I was able to recover my sense of self. This changed things for the better for me. One day I happened to tell a friend about the boy who had inadvertently saved my life.

"You should go back and see how he's doing," she urged. Soon after, I drove out to the development, taking the same route as before. I came to the same street, except there were no tidy rows of homes. No ranch house. Just a field of grass and trees. Yet I knew this had been the spot where the little boy lived. At least for that one day years ago when I needed him.

The Answer of My Life

Lauren Jackson

"DEAR HEAVENLY FATHER," I SCRAWLED, crouching in the dim hallway light at the top of the stairs. My diary looked blurry through my tears. I'd been waiting for a boy to call. I'd hoped he would ask me to the prom, but the phone never rang. At 2:00 AM I was wide awake and depressed. So I crawled out of the bedroom I shared with my sister and began a letter to God.

Fights with siblings, worries about school, issues with friends—I told God all of it. "Will a boy ever want to ask me out?" I wrote. "Will I always feel so unloved?"

I wondered if God would ever give me an answer. Just then a bright light illuminated the hallway, all the way to the bottom of the stairs. Within the bright, yellow light, I felt a strong presence. I heard a message: "You are loved beyond anything you could imagine."

A rush of love hit me. It was overwhelming. I ran from the light into the darkness of my bedroom, not sure exactly what to make of what I'd just seen and heard.

When I awoke the next morning, everything looked the same. My room, my house, my family—but something had changed. *I* was different: happy in the knowledge that I was so very precious to God. My diary had helped me ask God questions, and He had given me the most important answer of my life.

Midnight Visitors

Marianne Masterson

I HAVE WHAT? B CELL lymphoma? Cancer.

I know those words. I have worked for thirty years in San Antonio Health Center labs...looking at diseases and assisting in their diagnoses.

What about my kids? I want to be with my kids right now—whole, healthy, and strong, not sickly, useless, a burden. All the questions begin...But I eat healthy, I don't smoke, I don't drink. I exercise two frisky dogs every day after work. I am young...the new "thirty"...Why me?

I was in the hospital for a total of seventy-two grueling, pain-filled days. I was poked, prodded, and poked some more as I progressively lost weight. My lowest was eighty-two pounds. My face was sunken; my skin was hanging on my body. I couldn't eat. I couldn't sleep. I had IV lines and tubes everywhere, and I always seemed to end up on the sixth floor in the puke pink room....Oh yeah, I did a lot of that too. I was so nauseated from the chemo all the time.

My family has a long history of faith. My mom and dad were in church every Sunday along with us kids. But this ordeal was taking its toll on my spiritual as well as physical well-being. I admit there were moments in those horrific days I was ready to die.

Late into one painful night I woke up sensing someone was in the room with me. Sitting at the foot of my bed in the visitor chair was a young man. He didn't say anything. He just sat there serenely with me. I wasn't afraid; rather, I felt a sense of calm come over me and I drifted off to sleep.

A little later on I woke up. Instantly wide awake, I looked and, this time, sitting at the foot of my bed was an older woman. Again I wasn't afraid. She, too, had a sense of peace about her, and I felt comforted. I sensed, even though neither one spoke to me, that they were letting me know it was going to be okay. I could do this thing.

The next morning I called my aunt and recounted the experience. The first words out of her mouth were, "Marianne, I believe you were visited by angels. They came to give you encouragement."

It all made sense. Knowing that God sent angels just for me comforted me and helped me make it through this hard time and back to my life.

Counter Service

Daniel Frederick Fogarty

DUST ROSE OFF THE ROAD as I climbed down from the bus in Las Cruces, New Mexico. The air was sweltering, but it was a blessing to be here after the three-day bus ride. I picked up the small gunnysack that held my few possessions and looked around the town. Las Cruces in those days, deep in the Depression, wasn't the lively city it eventually became. But it was still a whole new world to me. The New Mexico desert was nothing at all like the lush pine forests of East Texas where I grew up. *What now?* I asked myself. I'd traveled hundreds of miles and spent the few dollars I had to come here, but I really didn't know where to go next. I'd come to New Mexico to find my father, but I had no idea where he might be.

I started to walk, not knowing where I was going. A few blocks from the depot, I spotted a neon sign flashing Open. A diner. My stomach rumbled. I hadn't eaten since I'd left Texas. I only had a few cents. Maybe enough for a cup of coffee. "That'll have to do," I muttered.

I pushed open the door to the diner and looked around at the other customers. I felt sure I would recognize my father, even though we hadn't seen each other in eleven years. I was seven then. My mother had just died. Dad didn't think he could care for me on his own and took me to the county orphanage. It was there that I last saw him.

"Have a seat, honey," a waitress behind the counter called to me. She was five feet tall at the most, but her smile was the biggest I'd ever seen.

Smiles weren't easy to come by in my life. Seemed like the workers at the orphanage were more interested in keeping kids in line than making us happy. I'd spent many years without getting even an orange for Christmas. I couldn't remember the last time I'd been welcomed so warmly.

I took a seat at the counter, thinking back on all those years I'd spent alone, planning my escape. A couple of times I'd even tried it with some of the older boys, slipping out of the orphanage at night and running. But each time the authorities caught us. They dragged us back to be punished. Like I said, it wasn't a place for smiles.

Glad I never have to go back there again, I thought. I was eighteen now. An adult. I could go wherever I wanted. And what I wanted—what I needed—was to find my father. I needed to see him one more time. I wanted to see him face-to-face.

The waitress came over, wiping her hands on her pink apron. "What can I get you?" she asked.

I'd planned to just ask for a cup of coffee, but she seemed so friendly, and it had been so long since I'd had someone to talk to. "I don't have much money," I said. "I just got off the bus. I'm from Texas." I dug in my pocket for the little change I had. "Would this get me a slice of pie? And maybe some coffee?"

The waitress looked down at the change in my hand. "Don't worry, honey," she said. "I'll be right back."

I sighed with relief. I had enough for pie. *What then?* I'd spent so long focused on getting to Las Cruces I hadn't thought about what I'd do when I got there. I didn't know where Dad lived. I didn't know anything about his life since he'd left me at the orphanage. A while back I'd gotten a visit from a distant relative and asked her about him. "I heard he's homesteading in New Mexico—Las Cruces, I think," she'd said.

"What's that?"

"Homesteading means he's got a parcel of land from the government. If he can find water on the land he gets to keep it. He has to prove there's water enough to plant—that means setting up a working well. To be honest, the odds are pretty slim for homesteaders out there. He might not have had any luck. But that's where I heard he might be."

It was all I had to go on. I don't know why I was so desperate to see him after he'd left us all behind. I just knew this was something I had to do. That is, if I even could do it. I looked around the diner again, filled with strangers' faces. How did I ever expect to find Dad here? New Mexico was a big place. I had no idea where my father's land claim was—if he still had it.

The waitress came back to the counter with a cup of coffee, a slice of pie, and the biggest sandwich I'd ever seen. The pie was topped with a big scoop of ice cream, which must have cost extra. "Oh, I can't…," I began.

"On the house," she said. "All of it."

I stared at the lady in her pink apron and thought she must truly be an angel. I wolfed down the sandwich. Then the pie. Each bite was like heaven. When I finished my coffee, my angel was there to refill it. "Thank you," I said.

"No problem," she said. "What brings you to Las Cruces?"

Might as well tell her, I thought. *Have to start searching somewhere!*

"I'm looking for someone," I said. "Ever heard of a John P. Fogarty?"

The smile that had been on her face since I walked in suddenly disappeared. Now she just looked surprised. "Why are you looking for him?"

"I'm his son," I said.

Her eyebrows rose. "If you wait until my shift is over, I'll take you to him," she said.

I thought I must have misheard her—could it be that easy? "You know my father?" I said. "How?"

"I'm Ora," she said. "I'm his wife!"

True to her word, that friendly waitress—my stepmother—took me home with her. That home became my home for more than a year. I helped Ora and my father develop their land until I left New Mexico to join the armed forces. During that time I got to know my father and understand why he'd done what he did. I forgave him for leaving us. Maybe that's the real reason I needed to find him after all.

It was no coincidence that I walked into that diner during Ora's shift. Angels guided my steps to New Mexico, just as they made sure Ora was waiting for me when I got there. Those angels have been guiding my steps ever since. From Texas to New Mexico, and everywhere I go.

CHAPTER 6

Sleep in Heavenly Peace

One Last Gift

Ellen Battipede Novack

VALENTINE'S DAY HAD COME AND gone, but there was one thing missing. *Lord, where is my ring?* I thought as I got ready for bed. My husband, John, had bought it for me before he died, but somehow he'd never given it to me. I glanced behind the bedroom door, where John's old blue robe still hung, the same place it had hung for our nearly twenty-six years of marriage. *How will you ever give me the ring now?* I wondered.

John loved to give presents. No matter how many times I told him I didn't need any fancy jewelry, he always found me something special. "It will make me happy to see you wear it," he always said.

I got into bed and turned out the light. John didn't need gold and silver to tell me that he loved me. His love was visible in the way he took care of me, our two daughters, and our granddaughter. On our last Valentine's Day together, he took me out for a romantic dinner. We held hands in the candlelight and reminisced about the past: our first date, the days our children were born, the birth of our granddaughter. He gave me a beautiful card and a bouquet of roses—but no jewelry. For the first time, it seemed John had actually listened to me.

Or so I thought, until I found that store receipt. I immediately knew when John had sneaked away to make a purchase. I'd returned from an errand to find the house empty, even though John's illness usually kept him at home. Just as I was really starting to worry, John walked in the front door. "Where were you?" I asked.

He wouldn't say, but it was so close to Valentine's Day, I had my suspicions. *I'll let him have his surprise*, I thought. But our Valentine's dinner was so wonderful I'd forgotten all about the mystery gift. John died soon after. Now I needed to know what had happened to John's surprise.

"Perhaps he ordered something and never got a chance to pick it up," I'd suggested to my daughter one day. We drove over to the store. She explained the situation to the manager.

"Of course I remember," he said. The manager opened a catalog and pointed to a picture of a ring with multiple stones. "It's a mother's ring," he said, "with a birthstone for each child. Your husband ordered three stones: alexandrite, garnet, and sapphire."

One for each of our daughters and one for our granddaughter. John had surprised me again. "Is the ring ready?"

"According to our records, it was already picked up," the manager said. He showed me the receipt, with John's signature at the bottom. John had definitely picked up the ring. But if he had picked it up, why hadn't he given it to me? Where was it now?

I tossed and turned in my bed. *Where is that ring?* I thought. Finally, I drifted off to sleep.

I dreamed I was in a car, looking out at the ocean. John was at my side. He looked as young and strong as he had when we first met. John gave me a fortune from a Chinese cookie. The fortune had my initials on it. "Turn it over," said John. "It's your claim ticket."

"For what?" I asked.

"The ring."

"But I went to the store and they said you picked it up."

John shook his head. "I'm picking it up on Saturday."

With that I woke up. I couldn't make sense of the dream, but seeing John again had filled me with joy. For the first time since his death I felt strong and ready to move forward with my life. There were things I couldn't put off any longer. Like donating John's clothes to Goodwill. I'd spend the week going through his wardrobe and ask my daughter to make the trip with me on Saturday. *I'm picking it up on Saturday*, John had said in the dream. But what did that mean?

By the time my daughter arrived to drive me over to Goodwill I had a pile of clothes ready. I'd gone through every pocket, emptied all John's closets and drawers. But I never came across a mother's ring with three stones. I did one final sweep of the bedroom closets before tying up the bags of clothing. "I've checked every item," I said. "It's just not here."

Saturday, John had said in the dream. Just like today. It was like a message I could not decipher.

I turned to leave the bedroom and something caught my eye. A flash of color on the back of the door. John's old robe, hanging on the hook where it had hung all those years. It was so familiar I hadn't remembered it. But looking at it now, I felt a rising excitement.

I slipped my hand into the left robe pocket. I felt the little square box. Inside was a ring with three sparkling stones: alexandrite, garnet, and sapphire.

John had surprised me again. He found a way to tell me he loved me, one last time, with one last gift, when I most needed to know it. I wear my ring every day. John's still taking care of us, with a little help from the angels.

A Sign to Let Me Know

Audrey Razgaitis

I'D BRUSHED MY TEETH, CHECKED my alarm clock, even rearranged my pillows—but I still couldn't sleep. *I won't be comfortable until I feel settled about Mom*, I thought. She'd died a week ago, but I was still so sad. *If only she could send me a sign or something*, I thought as I tossed and turned in bed. *Just a little sign, letting me know she's okay.*

My mother's last few years had been difficult. Heart disease made her weak and frail. Mom was an organized, no-nonsense woman, who raised five kids and found great joy in her five grandkids. She'd stayed active with lots of friends and hobbies, and loved the charity work she did for the Lithuanian National Foundation. As her health deteriorated, she had to give it all up. She'd had such a rough time those few years before she passed. All I wanted was to know that now she was happy in heaven.

I glanced at the clock: way too late! My husband was sound asleep beside me. It was time I got some rest too. I turned off my thoughts and closed my eyes.

The sound of the alarm clock usually made me grumpy, but the next morning when I heard the ring tone I smiled. I'd been dreaming one of those dreams that are almost more real than reality itself. Mom and I were in the car. I was driving her to a meeting at the Lithuanian National Foundation. She exuded a sense of expectation, of joy. She sat upright in the passenger seat, her cheeks full of color and life. I knew she didn't want to be late. To her, this was her most important work. We pulled into the parking lot right on time. As Mom climbed out of the car, I saw her dad, who had died fifteen years earlier. My grandfather was waiting near the building where Mom went for her meetings. Mom turned back toward me and waved. She looked happier and healthier than I'd seen her in years. Then she went to meet her father. And I had my sign.

When My Grandmother Called Us from Heaven

Alisa Edwards Smith

I WAS ELEVEN YEARS OLD and trying to sleep in my bed at Ogbomosho, Nigeria. Although I am an American, I spent most of my childhood in Nigeria, West Africa, because my parents were medical missionaries. My father, Dr. Keith Edwards, was a surgeon at Ogbomosho Baptist Hospital, and my mother, Alice Edwards, was an operating room nurse there.

My idyllic childhood changed when the Bifran War began. The Igbos, who lived in the eastern part of Nigeria, seceded from Nigeria and called themselves Bifran. At first I tried to ignore the war and pretend it did not exist. After all, most of the fighting was between the North and East and I lived in the west. But I began to notice that some of my Nigerian friends who were Igbo were disappearing. They were either being killed, or they were trying to leave and get back to the East (Bifra), where they would be safe.

On one particular night I lay in bed and thought about how my parents, like all the other missionaries, had bags packed in case the American Embassy called and told them that we were to be evacuated. I felt uncertain and unsafe for the first time in my life. The adult missionaries tried to pretend that everything was fine, but since most of the missionary kids, MKs as we were known, could understand Yoruba, we heard the tales of refugees being burned alive or killed. The adults were worried and short-tempered with us.

I began to have a recurring nightmare where I would wake up at the boarding school and everyone would be gone…evacuated…and they had forgotten me. I was left. Or I had a dream that we were all evacuated from school and all my friends were having happy reunions with their parents, but my parents and sisters were nowhere to be found.

As I lay awake I heard the telephone ring. Now you must realize that my father was a doctor and the phone had rung late many times before in our house when there was an emergency at the hospital. But for some reason this ring sounded slightly different to me. I sat up and got out of the bed and walked slowly toward my parents' bedroom.

I heard my father speaking softly. He sounded happy, somewhat urgent, and confused all at the same time. I heard him say, "Ma, how can this be you? How can you be calling me?" He laughed and said, "How can this be happening?" There was a pause and he was listening intently. Then I heard him say, "What is heaven like?" and another pause. Lastly, I heard him saying, "I will, Ma. I will hold tightly to God."

I was transfixed. I held on to the door frame to steady myself. Ma was my grandmother, my father's mother. I loved her, we all did, she was a wonderful woman and she had died when we were in America two years earlier. I remembered overhearing my father tell my mother how blessed he felt that God had allowed us to see her for that year and that he had been able to be by her bedside when she went home to heaven. I looked back into the room to see my father staring at the phone receiver. He then put the phone back on the hook, and I watched as he got out of bed, got on his knees by his bed, and prayed.

I went back to my bed and said my own prayers. I thanked God for sending Ma to call my father. I was old enough to know that he was operating on some of the victims of the war. I know he wondered if he was saving their lives only to have them killed later. I believed this haunted him and made him feel helpless. I climbed into my bed and slept.

The next day I asked my father what had happened the night before. He began to tell our family this incredible story. He told us that the phone had rung and he heard Ma's voice on the other end of the line. She told him that she loved him. He immediately asked how she could be calling him. My father paused, took a breath, and told us that his mother had said, "Keith, God sometimes allows us to reach across and help our loved ones when they are struggling." My father said she then said, "Keith, hold on to the Lord!" My father said he asked what heaven was like and she gently said, "I did not call to tell you that. I called to tell you to 'hold on to the Lord.' He knows of your struggles and He loves and cares about you." Then she was gone and he was left holding the phone in his hand.

I have discussed this incident with him many times since it happened. My father is a doctor, a man of science, and therefore he likes things that are explainable by science. Once he said, "Perhaps the phone rang by accident and my conversation with Ma was a dream. But even if it was, God speaks to His children through dreams all the time, and the end result is still the same. God spoke to me."

I know that the phone, in fact, rang because I heard it and went to my parents' bedroom. I believe it was not a dream; I think my beloved grandmother called my father on a night when both he and I needed her. We needed to be reminded that God is always in control no matter what. It does not matter what circumstance we find ourselves in—God is with us. And we need to do exactly what my grandmother said that night: "Hold on to the Lord!"

God reminds us that He is there for us, that, as it says in 1 Peter 5:7 (NIV), we are to "cast all [our] anxiety on him because he cares for [us]." A miracle happened that night: God healed our family's heart. And I will never forget that special night my grandmother called us from heaven!

Eternal Celebration

Kelly Smith

AFTER A HALF-DOZEN YEARS OF going to college during the days, coaching soccer in the evenings, and working in restaurants on the weekends, I had attained my goal. I had my first "real" job as a school psychologist in a residential treatment center for troubled adolescents, just outside of New York City.

But I wasn't able to entirely concentrate on my work. I hadn't been myself since my older brother had been killed. It was just nine months since Neil, at age thirty-two, had been hit and killed by a truck in our hometown of Dundee, Scotland. I had gone back for a month to be with my mom and dad after the accident, and, to tell the truth, my thoughts were still very much there, in the Scottish Highlands Neil loved, where we scattered his ashes.

The students I worked with each day came from painful circumstances full of violence, drug addiction, homelessness, and prison. My work involved assessing their progress and supporting them emotionally. I saw how hard it was for them to even envision a stable future when so few of them had ever experienced that kind of life. Their situation mirrored my circling thoughts about Neil. Although I had grown up in the Church of Scotland and knew what the Bible said about heaven, I could not envision it. I wondered, *Where is Neil? Is he happy? Does he even know that I got a job?*

One day, walking through the school on the way to my office, a teacher I knew only by face stopped me. He introduced himself as Chris and said, "I don't want you to be scared about what I am going to say. I had a dream last night that I know had something to do with you."

Stunned, I nodded for him to go on.

"In my dream I was in a crowded hall filled with long tables. There were people laughing, eating, and drinking together. I heard another language and there was music, but I can't remember what it sounded like. I was very aware of a certain young man there, with light brown hair and blue eyes. When I saw him, I had the strongest feeling that I needed to tell you about this dream.

"Do you know what this means?" Chris asked.

My brother? Like me, Neil had brown hair and blue eyes. I told Chris that my brother had died last year, and perhaps this was about him, somehow. But as to the setting of the dream, which seemed to be the main point, I couldn't make heads or tails of it. "Can you tell me any more?" I asked Chris.

"Well, the people were dressed funny," he said. "Kind of old-fashioned." A vision of men in breeches and suspenders popped into my mind, and women in full, long skirts and colorful, embroidered bodices. Oktoberfest!

I knew straightaway that Chris had seen a vision of Neil at Oktoberfest. This was my brother's favorite celebration, and he went to one in Germany every fall with his two best friends.

As I puzzled through the meaning of this dream, Jesus' words about heaven came to my mind: "In my Father's house are many mansions. . . . I go to prepare a place for you" (John 14:2, KJV). It had never occurred to me that heaven might be a bit different for each one of us—perhaps reflecting our favorite places here.

Chris and I still work together, and he has never had another dream about Neil. But from that day forward I have felt a peace about where Neil is. I'm engaged to be married, and I know that Neil is sharing my happiness at his own eternal celebration of God's goodness.

Mister Sunshine

Pam Bostwick

I WAKE UP IN A cold sweat and can't stop sobbing. The dream is so real: a child trapped, screaming that will not stop. It is me screaming. I cannot quit shaking while I pull the bedclothes around me. Restless, I can't go back to sleep. In the darkness I pray, "God, when will these nightmares end?"

There is no answer as I stumble from my bed and into the shower, to calm my nerves. It isn't morning yet. I must get away for a while to think. No, I don't want to think. The shadows of my past cling to me. No matter how I try, I can't cast away the burden of me as a child, abandoned, hurting.

I scrawl a note for my oldest daughter of five kids, telling her where I've gone. It being a Saturday, they will probably sleep until I return. I am a single mom.

I rush out the door and down the hill. "I can't take any more," I tell God. He already knows my pain, but I don't seem to reach Him somehow. I feel too desperate, too hopeless.

Recklessly, I half-walk, half-run for miles, it seems. I end up near my favorite lake. In the predawn I notice an old coupe parked there and groan inwardly. "Someone must be here this early when I'd like to be alone."

Light barely filters through the trees when I leave the car and slowly follow the path down to the stream bank.

I see a bald-headed man in ragged jeans and a faded sweatshirt crouching at the water's edge. For a fleeting second I wonder if he will accost me. *Should I leave?* Then he turns slightly and notices me. His features aren't striking. He's an ordinary man until he smiles. My fears dissolve as warmth floods through me. The sun isn't up, yet the heat of its rays flow from him. I stand rooted to the spot, transfixed.

"I leave you be and give you your space," he says.

"No," I answer, surprising myself. I thought I wanted my solitude. Now as I sit down on a large boulder not far from him, I add, "I'd like the company."

His serene manner brings tranquility to my troubled mind. His glowing countenance penetrates my aching heart like a healing balm.

He lays down his fishing pole and concentrates on the rocks before him. "Lookie, here's a pretty one, you can always find a pretty one." He grins at me and doesn't seem to mind me staring.

My eyes focus on the stones by him. "They all look like gray blobs to me in this gray dawn," I reflect. "Kind of like my life."

I realize he seems to be peering through me, and his look pierces my soul, but it doesn't frighten me or make me feel uncomfortable. I turn my hot face away to hide my unbidden emotion.

He walks over to me, reaches out his stub of a finger, and gently lifts my chin. I don't flinch or pull away. He wipes at a tear on my cheek. "There's lots of sadness in the world, and I'm sorry you be carryin' more than your share."

I wonder if there is a hurt in his old heart, since he seems to understand me so well. I can't speak through the lump in my throat. I have not received this kind of comfort in a long, long time. His whole being radiates a peace I had never known.

I had the urge to snuggle up next to him, to become a part of that assurance he seemed to possess within his entire self. He reminds me of a big, safe teddy bear. Who was he? Someone sent to rescue me from the harshness of my circumstances.

I long for his strong arms to steady me the way God tries to every day of my life if I would let Him. How could I have shut Him out?

I sweep my arm across the sky to take it all in. "I want to thank God for all this and embrace this new day with joy, not dread."

"Ya can't heal until ya get rid of the anger and bitterness," my companion acknowledges. Handing me a large stone, he motions for me to throw it into the depths below.

This is silly, I think to myself. To humor him I hurl the first stone into the river. It hits with a thud. Amazingly, I feel better.

Each time I thrust more rocks farther into the water, I imagine letting go of revenge toward my abusers. The agony of my own deep wounds seems to lift.

"The shame and guilt are gone," I exclaim in awe.

"The relief of getting rid of something pent up can give ya a solace ya have never known."

"And forgiveness," I whisper.

The exercise leaves me spent. I relax against a nearby tree and close my eyes.

Suddenly the sun peeps over the top of the hill and glimmers with hope, shattering the ice that had been in my heart for years.

"Jesus be here with you," the man states.

It is true. I know this with every fiber of my soul.

"Give that burden ya got to Him. He's strong enough and He's able to bear it for ya, and ya be a lot lighter feeling goin' home."

I feel a glow from this man, and believe he knows a great deal about Christ's love for me.

I squeeze my eyes shut while I picture God taking sacks filled with my darkness and garbage from me. As the weight and baggage and anguish I had packed around lifts from me, I offer up a prayer of gratitude to God.

I open my eyes and the man is gone. I blink in disbelief. Did he go through the woods, disappear, or what? I would never know, but his presence remains like a candle giving me faith.

I accept that the Lord has been here with me through this old man. God is not a stranger anymore. He knew I needed Jesus, with skin on. I would never have this same despair again. That day in the mountains my life was impacted forever by an angel unaware.

Blessed by the Angels

Maureen Heintz

BILL AND I LOST OUR nineteen-day-old son, Dylan Patrick, due to high-risk
pregnancy complications.

Five-and-a-half years later, we were the parents of two beautiful boys, Nolan,
four, and Jack, three, when I had a very clear and vivid dream. I was sitting with
my father, "Old Man Jack," who was deceased, showing him my paintings. (I am
not a painter.) There was a knock at the door, and my father and I heard a voice.
"Special delivery! Special delivery for Maureen!"

I said to my father, "Who could that be?"

He turned to me with a twinkle in his eye and answered, "Why don't you go
answer and see?"

When I opened the front door, there was a man all in white. He was carrying
two long white boxes tied with white ribbons. "Who is this for?" I asked the man.

"Why this is for you, my child," he replied. "This is your blessing!"

When I opened the first box, there were dozens and dozens of long white
roses with a spectacular crystal shine to them. The card inside said: "I am sorry
that it did not work out the way you wanted it to the first time, but I will always be
with you and love you."

The second box had a beautiful baby girl in a full-lace white gown and a lace bonnet. "Whose baby is this?" I asked.

"This is your baby," the man said. "You can keep her and love her with all of your heart."

Two weeks later, I was pregnant with our fourth child, and I knew it was a girl. Even with the knowledge of being high-risk, I did not worry at all during this pregnancy.

After nine months of a normal pregnancy, Julia was born. Our doctor was in total shock at what he saw. First, the umbilical cord was looped around the baby's neck twice; he questioned how she was not strangled to death in the womb. Second, there were two very tight knots in the umbilical cord, so the doctor wondered how the baby had not starved to death and how she had received any nutrition at all.

When Julia was a baby, before she spoke her first words, Bill and I would stand near her nursery and listen to her. It was like she was singing with angels! I knew she was truly a blessing, and as Julia grew, everyone she came in contact with would say, "What a lovely angel she is!" As a teenager, she still is.

I truly believe there are angels who come to us in our dreams to support us. We just need to be open to their guidance.

Hope in the Afterlife

Norman Vincent Peale

MY FATHER, WHO DIED AT eighty-five after a distinguished career as a physician and minister, had struggled against a very real fear of death. But after his funeral, my stepmother dreamed that he came to her and said, "Don't ever worry about dying. There's nothing to it!" The dream was so vivid that she woke up, astounded. And I believe that he did come to reassure her, because that is precisely the phrase I had heard him use a thousand times to dismiss something as unimportant.

Years before, when news reached me that my mother had died, I was alone in my office, numb with grief. There was a Bible on my desk, and I put my hand on it, staring blindly out the window. As I did so, I felt a pair of hands touch my head, gently, lovingly, unmistakably. Was it an illusion? A hallucination? I don't think so. I think my mother was permitted to reach across the gulf of death to touch and reassure me.

Once when I was preaching at a big church convocation in Georgia, I had the most startling experience of all. At the end, the presiding bishop asked all the ministers in the audience to come forward and sing a hymn.

Watching them come down the aisles, I suddenly saw my father among them. I saw him as plainly as when he was alive. He seemed about forty, vital and handsome, singing with the others. When he smiled at me and put up his hand in an old familiar gesture, for several unforgettable seconds it was as if my father and I were alone in that big auditorium. Then he was gone. But he was there, and I know that someday, somewhere, I'll meet him again.

Vision of God's Love

Joan Wester Anderson

JIM SNYDER WOULD CONSIDER HIMSELF an ordinary man living an ordinary life, surely not one that involves angel sightings. But when his young wife died of pancreatic cancer, Jim was devastated by her loss. He tried to hold everything together and deal with his grief. But as months passed and Jim's heartache continued, "I began asking God for a sign that everything would be okay, and that I would eventually get through this," Jim says. One night, about six months after his loss, as he lay in bed trying to fall asleep, he opened his eyes for a moment. There, floating almost casually above his bed was an angel. "The image was moving, and the face of the angel was surrounded by pillow-white clouds, almost like a wreath," Jim recalls.

Jim could scarcely believe what he was seeing. He blinked several times, but the vision remained. Then slowly it moved across the ceiling. "It had the most peaceful look on its face," Jim says, "and it slowly faded away. I lay there for several minutes, enjoying the calmest and most restful feeling I had ever experienced."

Jim thought about the vision all week. Was it an angel? If so, why had it been sent to him? He was just an ordinary person, wasn't he? Perhaps it had just been a figment of his imagination? And yet there had been that indescribable moment of joy and unshakable faith....

That Wednesday, Jim attended a Bible study meeting and also went to church services. As the groups broke up and people headed home, Jim asked the Bible instructor, a complete stranger, if they could speak privately. "I told him what had happened," Jim says. "I wanted to know if he thought I was going crazy, or perhaps seeing things that weren't there."

The man smiled, as if he were not at all surprised by Jim's words. He walked to his books lying on the table and picked up his Bible. Turning to a marked page, he handed the Bible to Jim. "I noted this over twenty years ago," he said, "when I saw an image very much like the one you're describing."

Jim could hardly believe it. He looked at the underlined text. "And an angel appeared to him from heaven, and comforted him" (Luke 22:43, wyc). The brief verse described Jesus' suffering in the garden before His crucifixion.

Jim was flooded with understanding. God had not sent an angel to banish His own Son's pain, or even to lift it, for this was not in the heavenly plan. But God had sent an angel—to His Son and to every grieving person—to simply be there, with comfort and understanding. "Life is sometimes difficult," Jim's angel had been telling him, "but you will never go through it alone."

The Angel of Hope

Lorna Byrne

I HAVE BEEN SEEING AND talking with angels since I was a little baby. I see angels every day, and I see them physically, just as I see someone sitting in front of me. Angels are my friends and companions, and I talk with them all the time, sometimes using words and sometimes without words. I have no idea why I should be able to see angels and you don't. I'm just an ordinary person.

I had seen the Angel of Hope previously, but this day when I was twelve was the first time that I learned who this particular angel was and how he helps us.

The Angel of Hope doesn't look like any other angel I have ever seen. He looks like a massive flame. Within this very bright flame, I am shown a faint human appearance, which is masculine, and a beautiful, dazzling emerald-green color, holding a torch—like an Olympic flame. The brightness of the Angel of Hope looks different from any other angel; I think this is because it's a light within a light.

The Angel of Hope is enormous, the height of a mature tree. When I see him, he always seems to be very far away from me. So he should then look small, but he's always massive. It's quite strange—it's as if he's very far away but right in front of me at the same time, hard as that is to explain.

He seems to be forever moving, turning back constantly to encourage whoever he is leading at the time with a gentle smile. His expression is one of love and encouragement.

Lately I have been seeing the Angel of Hope a lot more than I would have previously. I probably see him every day. People seem to be needing hope so much at this time.

All those years ago, the angel showed me a vision of the Angel of Hope at work, so that I could understand more about him. I was shown the Angel of Hope guiding soldiers through a trench battlefield. I have no idea what nationality the soldiers were. I was shown one particular soldier crawling exhausted through the mud. I could see he was injured. The Angel of Hope was moving in front of him, constantly beckoning him forward. I was allowed to see through the soldier's eyes. The soldier could not see the Angel of Hope, but he saw a light, and within this light the soldier could see those he loved—his wife and young children, his elderly parents. The Angel of Hope was giving him the strength to stay alive, encouraging him not to give up, by giving him hope of a reunion with the family he loved.

"Do you understand, Lorna?" the angel said. "The Angel of Hope can't stop the war, heal this soldier, or rescue him, but he can give him the strength to make it to where he can be rescued." The angel smiled at me and continued. "That soldier died in his bed many years later." I was so pleased with this news. The love that the young soldier had for his family was very beautiful.

SPECIAL SECTION

All Creatures Great and Small

A Butterfly Kiss

Barbara Wills

I SAT ON THE PORCH remembering how my son Lee used to hold my hand on walks, snuggle with me while we read books together, and even exchange secret winks in the hallway when I was a substitute teacher at his school. Tomorrow would be the anniversary of his sudden death, at nine years old. My husband and I saved keepsakes from Lee around the house to keep him close, but at times like these, mementos were nothing compared to feeling like he was really here with me. *God, I need to know my bond with Lee is still strong even though he is in heaven.*

A flicker of motion near a pot of petunias caught my eye. A tiny, pale blue butterfly, no bigger than my thumbnail, moved from bloom to bloom. *Strange,* I thought. *I've never seen a butterfly like that before.* I watched as the creature fluttered over to me. I extended my index finger. The butterfly landed on it! The butterfly flitted away, only to return to my fingertip again and again, as if playing a game. Finally my winged friend flew up to the bridge of my nose and rested there. I held still, hoping to prolong the magic of being eye-to-eye with a butterfly! Seconds later the creature flew away, never to be seen again.

What had just happened? I sat dazed for several minutes before heading inside. On the refrigerator, among many family photos, I noticed a faded paper butterfly. Lee had given it to me one Mother's Day. Tears flowed from my eyes as I read the words written there: "Butterfly, go to my mother and whisper that I love her." Now I understood. God had answered my prayer with a beautiful message delivered on the wings of one of His most heavenly creatures.

Message of the Bobcat
Sandi Olson

"YOU SHALL MOUNT UP WITH wings as eagles. You'll run and not be weary." The words came from one of my favorite verses, from Isaiah (40:31), but why they came to me as I looked out the window that winter morning, I didn't know. I wanted nothing more than to stay inside underneath the covers. But I had to go out for a walk.

Just a week before, I was in the ICU, flat on my back recovering from heart surgery. I couldn't even get out of bed. Then I progressed to taking a few steps, leaning on my husband, Doug. It was a relief when the doctor said I could go home, but he gave me strict instructions.

"You need to exercise to get your strength up," he'd explained when he discharged me. "I'm prescribing a daily walk. Any distance is good at first. Once you get used to it, you can challenge yourself by walking a little farther each day."

I'd agreed to the program—anything to go home. But now I wasn't sure I could follow through with it. Getting dressed had exhausted me. "You can do it," Doug said, opening the door for me. "The sooner you start, the sooner it will get easier."

I stepped outside and shivered in the wintry breeze. Again came the verse from Isaiah: *"You shall run and not be weary."* Doug was the runner in our family.

And my days of running around the tennis court seemed like another lifetime. "Come on," Doug said. "One foot in front of the other."

Somehow I made it around the block. I returned home nearly as tired as I'd been right after the surgery. Doug helped me onto the couch. "Don't get discouraged," he said. "Tomorrow will be better."

Tomorrow? I couldn't imagine exerting this much effort again so soon. How weak I still was! Doug was trying his best, but his encouragement wasn't enough.

"Maybe you can set yourself goals," said Doug. "That's what runners do. Try to get to that meadow on the edge of the neighborhood."

I'd need an angel to carry me. No way could I get that far on my own. Before my surgery I'd barely noticed the grassy meadow only blocks from our house, a peaceful, open space dotted with wildflowers, tall tufted hairgrass bobbing in the breeze. Now that short walk might as well have been a marathon. Still, I had to walk somewhere. Every day I trudged a few steps more, closer to my goal, my legs so heavy it was as if they were filled with lead.

In two weeks' time I stood at the edge of the meadow, breathing hard. *I got here,* I thought, *but I don't have the strength to enjoy it.* I considered the words from Isaiah. Mount up with wings? Hardly.

I was about to turn to go home when a movement caught my eye. I stood stock-still, staring. Was it just the wind moving the tall blades? No. Something was moving in the grass—something big. Through the blades a tail flicked. Two pointed ears sailed above the grass. Then, just a few yards away, in clear sight, appeared the noble face of a bobcat. I caught my breath. A bobcat!

I wasn't frightened, despite how close the animal was. I was stunned by its power and beauty. I'd never seen a bobcat before, especially not in our residential neighborhood. But there was no denying the one in front of me. I watched in awe, marveling at the strength of his muscular body, until the bobcat turned and slipped away in the grass. In the quiet I realized that my breathing had slowed. My legs no longer felt like lead. Perhaps it had done me good to stop and rest. But as I stepped into the meadow where the bobcat had been, I felt more than just rested. I felt rejuvenated. For the first time since my operation I enjoyed the sensation of walking. The crisp air on my skin, the swish of the grass against my legs, the strain of my muscles. To *"run and not be weary..."* I almost remembered what that felt like.

The next day I had no trouble getting out of bed. "You're early this morning," said Doug when I pulled on my jacket for my walk.

I glanced up at the clock. "I guess I am," I said. I hadn't told Doug of my accomplishment in case it was a fluke. I wasn't sure my newfound energy was here to stay. But now I felt more confident. "I finally got to the meadow yesterday," I said. "I'm going to walk back there today."

I took my time, enjoying the sights and sounds along the way. What awaits me today? I wondered.

At the edge of the meadow, I scanned the tall grass. There was no sign of the bobcat, but I felt his presence as I walked around. It was almost as if he were watching me, encouraging me in my recovery, reminding me that God made all His creatures strong. Including me. I returned to the meadow every day, reciting Isaiah 40:31 as I walked: "They that wait upon the LORD shall renew their strength; they shall mount up with wings as eagles...." I didn't see the bobcat on my visits, but walking had become a reward in itself. I held on to Isaiah's promise. Together, Doug and I explored areas far beyond the meadow, and the chilly days of winter gave way to spring, then summer, then fall—until it was winter again. Exactly a year from that first day I made it to the meadow. It seemed only right to celebrate by returning there that morning.

Thank You, God, I thought as I gazed out on the familiar trees, grass, and... what was that? Something moving. Something big. A tawny tail appeared above the blades. The bobcat raised its head and looked at me, almost as if he knew I would come.

Thank you too, I thought. The Lord had sent an angel to carry me after all.

The Mangy Angel

Esther L. Vogt

COLD MARCH SHOWERS PELTED MY face as I stepped from the warmth of the church and threaded my way across the lot toward the parsonage.

Thursday evening's meeting of the women's missionary society had finally closed, and as the pastor's wife, I was the last to leave.

My husband had gone to a general conference in Detroit, and the children and I were alone. I half-expected to find the parsonage cloaked with night, for the hour was late and the children should have been in bed hours ago.

Letting myself in quietly, I was surprised to find the kitchen light still burning. Ted, our oldest, his dark head bent over his books, was studying at the table. He looked up as I came in.

"H'lo, Mom. Wet out, isn't it?"

"It's a wild night, all right," I said wryly, peeling off my dripping coat and boots.

He went back to his homework.

As I turned to leave the kitchen I looked down. Then I gasped. Our huge, mangy dog lay stretched out at Ted's side!

"Ted! What's Brownie doing in the house?" I demanded. "You know he's never stayed inside before!"

Ted glanced up from his book and shrugged. "Why, he just wanted in so I let him in. Then I decided I might as well bring my homework down here."

Brownie wanted in! That, in itself, was utterly incongruous. For that matter, so was everything else about that dog.

Black, brown, and smelly—and of undetermined breed—he had wandered to the parsonage one day and simply decided to stay. He adopted our family and was fiercely protective of us in every way. In fact, he loved us so much that he wanted to be where we were. Yet, once we'd let him into the house, he developed a peculiar claustrophobic streak. He would race in terror from window to door to window until we'd let him out. No amount of bribing or petting could persuade Brownie to remain indoors. Even the dreary *drip-drip* of rain from the eaves failed to lure him inside. He preferred the most inclement outdoor weather to being enclosed.

Until now.

There he was, lying calmly beside Ted in the kitchen like a very ordinary house dog.

I remembered his previous fierce possessiveness of us. Our large, redbrick parsonage sprawled comfortably on a big grassy plot behind the church and opposite the public school. Children often cut across the church property and through our yard when hurrying to and from school. We didn't mind. In fact, they were our friends. Against our better judgment, we often had report cards thrust at us even before parents saw them.

That is, until the dog came. He growled threateningly at anyone who dared cross our yard. Yet Brownie always came when I called him off.

Still, with people dropping in at our parsonage at all hours of the day, I was afraid someday I wouldn't get him called off in time.

I tried desperately to find another home for him, but with no success. Once I even called the Humane Society.

"Sure, lady," they said. "We'll get him. But you gotta catch him and shut him up for us."

Shut Brownie up? Impossible! One might as well try to imprison a victim of claustrophobia in an elevator! Until a better solution presented itself, he would have to remain with us.

And that's how things stood that wild, stormy night I came home from church.

Shaking my head at Brownie's strange behavior, I went down to the basement to bolt the door that leads to the outside. I came back up directly and retired to the living room with the paper.

Ted already had gone up to bed, and I decided to turn in too. The dog still lay on the kitchen floor, his shaggy head resting on his front paws.

Better put Brownie out first, I thought as I entered the kitchen to lock the back door. Rain still drummed steadily against the windows.

But when I tried to get the dog out of the door, he refused to budge. I wheedled; I coaxed. I pushed and pulled. He remained stationary.

Going to the refrigerator, I took out a chunk of meat and tried to bribe him to the door by dangling it in front of him. He still refused to move.

With a bewildered sigh, I picked up his hind end, yanked him toward the door, and out of it. Like quicksilver, his front end slid back in!

I grabbed his front end, and the back was in. His four feet seemed like a baker's dozen. Stubborn, determined, yet somehow placid. Talk about Balaam's donkey— I knew exactly how Balaam felt!

Should I call Ted to help me? No, the hour was late and Ted needed his sleep. I decided to shut all the doors to the kitchen and leave the dog inside. Then I went wearily to bed.

The next morning the dog reverted to his true nature and frantically tore out of the house.

A puzzled frown ribbed my forehead as I went down to the basement to turn on the furnace. What had made Brownie behave so strangely? Why had he been determined to remain in the house this one particular night? I shook my head. There seemed to be no answer.

When I reached the bottom of the stairs, I felt a breath of cold, damp air. Then a queer, slimy feeling swept over me. The outside door was open! Was someone in the basement?

After the first wave of panic had drained from me, my reasoning returned. Someone had gone out of the basement!

Limp with the reality of that fact, I looked around. The windows were as snug and tight on the inside as ever. Whoever had gone out of that door had been in when I had gone down to bolt it the night before! He apparently had heard my unsuccessful attempts to put the dog out and knew he had to come up through the kitchen and face the dog—or go out the door he had come in earlier.

That smelly, stray pooch had known this, and God had used him to keep us safe. Why didn't he growl or bark? I don't know. Maybe he knew he didn't have to.

I had always believed that God has definite work for His holy angels, and that as His child I could lay claim to the verse in Hebrews 1:14 (KJV): "Are they [angels] not all ministering spirits, sent forth to minister for them who shall be heirs of salvation?"

But His "ministering spirit" had taken a peculiar form that wild, stormy night. Instead of glorious, dazzling wings, the Lord had given our guardian angel four stubborn, mangy feet!

In Silent Song

Sophy Burnham

MY FRIEND'S BELOVED AND AGED dog died not long ago. My friend was in a state of grief and there I sat helpless to comfort her—for what can assuage the loss of a dog, a cat, a horse, mouse, parrot, or pet snake? Our animal relationships are pregnant with meaning and almost as profound as the loss of a child. Where do our animals go when they die?

I remember when Puck, my Corgi, died. For weeks afterward I could hear the click of his nails on the bare wood floors, as if he were still following me through the house. I missed him with a physical ache, the way he'd throw himself at the front door each noon to protest the mail that attacked through the brass slot (his ferocity succeeded, for didn't the invader retreat after Puck's assault, only to return the next day?). How could such life-force energy just disappear?

The fact that I could hear my dog's nails on the floor disturbed me. Was it my imagination, forged in the fires of grief? And how was it that after two or three weeks it faded out and stopped?

In Colorado once I was giving a talk on angels, when a woman asked: "Do dogs become angels when they die?" Then she told the following story:

She'd had a beautiful Shetland sheepdog in Idaho. It wore a red bandanna around its neck, a hippie dog. When it died, she fell into a depression—inconsolable.

She finally withdrew to a retreat center on the top of a mountain in New Mexico, where she spent her days reading, praying, walking, and recovering from her loss.

One day she was hiking in the high mountains when a thunderstorm broke overhead. Lightning flashed. She knew she was in danger. Some fifty-five people a year are killed by lightning in the United States and those deaths are most prevalent in the high mountains. The woman had a poor sense of direction, and while hurrying to reach the safety of the retreat, she got lost. She was scared. Suddenly she heard a bark. She looked up. Through the rain she saw a Shetland sheepdog with a red bandanna around its neck, running back and forth ahead of her. When she took a step toward it, the dog ran down a path. If she hesitated, it came back, barking, inviting her to follow. As it ran down the slope ahead of her, she saw the dog's plumy tail waving in great circles, like a pinwheel, just as her dog's used to do. The dog led her to her own cabin at the retreat, turned, and ran away.

Was it her dog? Was it an angel? I have been privileged to know one perfect loving dog, one perfect cat, and now an exceptional horse, each one the full expression of unflinching love. I think our animals are angels, earth-angels, pointing out for us the steadfast path of love, loyalty, optimism, faith, joy, hope. They teach us everything important about life.

And when we grieve their deaths, it is love that we're expressing in silent song—our grief being a poem proportionate to our love.

Angel by My Side

Hazel Houston

ONE DAY A DOG APPEARED at our farm. Somehow we understood that he had come to stay. We fed him table scraps, but he did not beg for food as some dogs do, nor did he wag his tail with happiness when fed.

He did not have a distinctive coloring. His hair was brown mixed with black, his tail stubby. We did not even give him a name, perhaps because he never had to be called. He was always there. This dog seemed to think his mission in life was to accompany me as I went about the outdoor duties of a farmwife. When I fed the chickens or gathered vegetables, he was by my side. Sometimes, not only did he escort me, but he also carried one of my hands gently in his mouth.

One day a stranger came. Oddly, he parked his car midway between the house and barn. When I stepped out on the porch, he asked a question about the previous owner of our farm. Then he appeared not to hear my answer. He walked toward me and asked the question again. This time I walked out in the yard a short way before I answered him. Again he seemed not to understand and continued to walk toward me. Now I sensed that he could hear me perfectly well.

Suddenly the man came to an abrupt stop. "Will that dog bite?" he asked.

I had not realized the dog was beside me, so quietly had he come. This time he did not take my hand in his mouth. His upper lip was pulled back, revealing sharp teeth.

"He certainly will," I answered firmly.

The man understood my words perfectly. He hurried to his car and drove away.

Soon after, the dog left. He may have gone to hunt rabbits and just never have come back.

Somehow I do not think so.

Out of the Night

Jack Haring

CHRISTMAS DAY 1944

Dear Mom:

This is a very different Christmas Day than I have ever spent in my life. Right now I'm living in the hayloft of a farmer's barn, and yet I'm glad to be here rather than out in a foxhole somewhere....

The Battle of the Bulge. The final desperate attempt of the Germans to break through Allied lines in Belgium and dash to Antwerp and the sea. For six days our 84th Infantry Division had been diverted from the Ninth Army in the north to the beleaguered First Army area in the Ardennes forest. The fiercest fighting of the war, and I, a nineteen-year-old private, was in the middle of it.

My letter home to Pennsylvania was written on a Christmas morning that was sunny and quiet—deceptively quiet. "The barn I slept in last night," I wrote, "made me think of the place where Jesus came into the world." Then I began reminiscing to Mom about the good Christmases we'd had as I was growing up—always starting with the traditional dawn service at St. John's Lutheran in Boyertown. Church had always been an important part of my life. I'd started college thinking I might go into the ministry.

The letter home was upbeat all the way. I didn't mention anything about the things that had been troubling me. How I had become disillusioned with organized religion because I saw so few Christians either at home or in the combat zone—certainly not Christians trying to live the way Jesus had taught. Or how the weather had been so miserable and the fighting so blazing that I feared I'd never live to see Pennsylvania again.

The last straw was being sent to these snow-covered hills and woods where we might be attacked at any moment from out there, somewhere. I was beginning to think that God had forsaken me.

Still, even though we'd spent the last five days floundering around trying to stop the Germans, even though our supply trucks had been captured, at least we'd had a barn for shelter on Christmas Eve, and our cooks were promising us a hot meal for Christmas Day.

"Let's go, men," Sergeant Presto, our squad leader, shouted. "Collect your gear and fall out. We're going on a mission."

I groaned. We all groaned. There went our first hot meal in a week!

We drove for about ten miles and then the trucks dropped us and sped away. It was dusk. Troops were strung out all along a dirt road that circled through some hills. When Presto came back from a meeting with the platoon leader, he gathered the ten of us—we were one man short in the squad—around him.

"Okay, men, here's what we're going to do. This won't take long and we're going to travel light. Leave your packs and entrenching tools here." He made it sound so simple. Intelligence had said that some German infantry were dug into a nearby hill and were causing havoc by shooting down on the roads in the area. Our battalion's job was to go up and flush them out.

Single file on each side of the winding road, we moved up the hill. We moved quietly, warily. At the top, we were surprised to find, not Germans, but an abandoned chateau in the middle of a clearing. Our squad went into the building. We found a billiard table and the tension broke as we played an imaginary game of pool using our rifles as cues.

Then Presto came stalking in. The Germans, he said, were in the woods beyond the clearing. Our orders were to chase them out into the waiting arms of another battalion positioned at the other end of the woods.

"There'll be three companies in this deal," Presto said. "Two of us will stretch out along the edge of the forest while the other hangs back in reserve. Now, as soon as we push into the woods, everybody fires, got it?"

We spread out, walked through the darkness to the forest's edge, then, at a signal, we burst in, opening up with everything we had. We kept up a brisk pace, keeping contact with our buddies along the moving line, walking and firing for about a mile. But the forest was empty. There was no movement...

The trees in front of us exploded. Suddenly, the night went bright with every kind of firing I'd ever seen or heard of—rifles, rifle-launched grenades, mortars, machine guns, tracers over our heads, bullets at our thighs. But worst of all, Tiger tanks. At least six of them, opening up point-blank with 88-millimeter cannons. Their projectiles whined and crashed all up and down our line.

Our intelligence was wrong, I thought angrily, as I flung myself down on my stomach. They told us there were no tanks up here. Now we were really in for it.

Within seconds men were screaming in pain all around me. I saw a tree with a big trunk and made a sudden lunge to get behind it, but I wasn't quick enough. Something tore into my thigh. There was hot, searing pain.

We were completely pinned down. The Tiger tanks kept scanning their turrets and firing on every yard of our line. The German ground troops sent their small-arms fire into anything that moved.

The minutes went by. Five. Ten. Fifteen. Then came a lull in the barrage. I called over to my best buddy, Kane. We called him "Killer." He was the gentlest guy in our platoon, but we'd nicknamed him that after the popular comic strip character "Killer Kane."

"Are you hurt, Killer?"

"Naw. But I think everybody else over here is. Presto's hit bad."

I called to Cruz on my right. He was our squad's BAR (Browning automatic rifle) man. There was no answer. Then I barely heard him whispering, "I'm hurt. Real bad. Floyd's dead. Corporal John's hit bad."

Well, I thought, *if Presto's out and the corporal, too, we don't have a leader.*

The pounding started again, this time with flares so they could spot us better. We did some firing back, and then the action subsided into another lull.

Down along the rear of our line came a figure, crawling. It was our platoon runner. "Captain says we're getting nowhere," he whispered to Killer and me. "We're pulling back in five minutes. Move out when you hear our covering fire."

I crawled over to Killer. "We've got to get our guys out of here," I said. "You go up your side and I'll go down mine, and we'll drag as many as possible to that big tree back there."

"How're we going to get them out of here, though?"

"I don't know," I said. "But we can't leave them lying here."

We were trapped. I lay there on the cold ground feeling helpless, that forsaken feeling again. Where was the God that I had prayed to during all those years of church and Sunday school back home in Pennsylvania? "And whatsoever ye shall ask in my name, that will I do," the Bible had said to me clearly (John 14:13, KJV). Was it necessary, when I needed help so badly, to ask?

"Oh, Lord," I mumbled, "help us. We're trying to get our wounded buddies out of here. Show us the way."

I had no sooner started dragging Corporal John toward our meeting tree when the firing started up in the center of our line. *There's the signal for pulling back*, I thought frantically, *but we can't do it. The Germans will sweep in on us; they'll mop us up before we can pull back.*

Just as I got to the tree, I saw that Killer had brought back three wounded squad members. So we had six in all to get back. I closed my eyes and in desperation said: "In Your name, Lord, help us."

I opened my eyes. In the black of night, moving mysteriously among the shattered trees, a giant hulk came toward us. *The Germans*, my heart thumped, *they've broken out of the brush. They're bearing down on us.* No, it was something else, something unbelievable. It now came into full view and stopped beside our tree.

A horse.

A big, docile, shaggy chestnut, standing there without a harness, as though awaiting our bidding.

Killer and I looked at each other in disbelief. We didn't question then where the horse came from, or how, or why; we just got to work. Moving swiftly, we draped Cruz and the corporal on the chestnut's broad back, then Mike and Presto. Then, with Killer carrying one of our buddies and me carrying the other, we led the horse out of the woods. At the clearing the horse trotted on ahead of us, straight to the chateau, and by the time Killer and I got there, our wounded were already on medical stretchers. The two men we carried in were cared for; the medics gave a quick look at my shrapnel wound; and then, as fast as we could, Killer and I went to find the horse. We wanted to pat him, give him some sugar, anything to make him sense our gratitude.

But he wasn't there. We looked everywhere, asked everyone we saw, but no one could tell us anything about him. He had simply vanished—gone from us as mysteriously as he had come.

The next morning at the aid station the shrapnel was removed from my leg, and at noon Killer and I lined up for our belated Christmas dinner. The day before, 190 men in our company would have answered the chow call; today there were thirty-five of us. All the wounded men in our squad had survived, however, though some were never to see action again.

Killer and I looked at the turkey and sweet potatoes in our mess kits. Hot and savory and long-awaited as this food was, we had no appetite. We were still too full of our emotions: the sorrow for lost buddies; the shock of our own survival; the strange, deeply affecting arrival and departure of the horse. We could not get the horse out of our minds then, nor have I since, for that noble creature did more than just save our lives; he reaffirmed my faith. I have always believed that on that Christmas night, God sent that horse to reassure a doubting soldier of His presence, even as He had sent His Son for that purpose on a Christmas night twenty centuries ago.

Good Boy, Floyd Henry

Carol Witcher

DOGS HAVE ALWAYS HELD A special place in my heart. Where others might just see an animal, I see a part of my family. So when my boxer, Floyd Henry, came up to me one evening while I was sitting on the sofa, I put down my novel and leaned in to give him a hug. "Come here, boy," I said, holding out my arms. He put his paws up on the sofa cushion and settled into my embrace. But then he reared his big square head. "What is it?" I asked. "What's got you startled?"

Floyd Henry regarded me with a questioning expression. *This is odd.* Floyd Henry had never given me such a concerned look before. Not in all of the five years we'd been together. He sniffed at my nose and mouth. Then he snapped his teeth in my face.

"Hey!" I yelled. I couldn't believe what had just happened. Floyd Henry was in no way, shape, or form aggressive. And we didn't ever play rough. I took his head in my hands, gently but firmly. "No!" I said. "We don't do that."

Floyd Henry didn't back down. Again, he snapped at my face. "Bad boy!" I said harshly, although it pained me to do it. I never had occasion to speak to him that way. I pushed his paws back down onto the carpet. "Go lie down," I told him.

Floyd Henry trotted off. I picked up my book and settled back into the sofa. But I couldn't relax. There had to be a logical explanation for Floyd Henry's behavior. *Was he trying to grab food I dropped on myself at dinner? Was he scared of something?* My loving companion wasn't making sense.

In a way, the very beginning of our relationship didn't make any sense either. I hadn't been looking for a dog when I bought Floyd Henry. I noticed an ad in the classified section of the newspaper: "Boxer for sale." I flipped the page and sipped my coffee. I certainly didn't need another dog. Since retiring from teaching I'd been fostering boxer dogs in my home. Many came to me with physical limitations and emotional scars. I was determined to help them overcome their problems. When I was a teacher, I taught all of my students that they were special and had a reason to be on this earth. I believed the same for my dogs.

One of my charges laid his chin on my knee as I browsed the rest of the classifieds that day. My mind kept going back to that tiny ad. I turned back. *Boxer for sale.* With so many dogs already counting on me, why was I even giving the advertisement a second thought?

Curiosity welled up inside me. I wanted to know this dog's story. Why was he being sold? Where would he go? I gave in and made the phone call. A man answered, and we arranged to meet later that day.

I heard barking as soon as I stepped out of my car onto the property. The storm door opened and a puppy ran out, his tail wagging. The man of the house shook my hand. "My daughter brought the puppy home," he explained. "But then she went off to college. My wife and I were looking forward to traveling now that we have an empty nest, and we just can't keep him."

Looks like I'm getting another dog after all. For whatever reason, God had put us together. We loved each other—so why was he snapping at me? I watched Floyd Henry settle onto his bed for a nap. I tried to put the incident out of my mind.

But Floyd Henry's odd behavior continued. He furiously sniffed at my breath and snorted loudly whenever I leaned in close to him. Four days after he initially snapped at my face, I leaned in for another hug. He swung his head sharply and bumped my right breast with his nose. Hard.

"Ouch!" The pain was so intense I had to take a breath to get my bearings. Why was my breast so tender? That day I scheduled a mammogram.

"Ms. Witcher," the surgical oncologist said after examining the results, "there's a mass in your right breast. We can give you a breath test to learn more." All I had to do was puff air into a small cylindrical tube. The organic compounds in my breath were then tested in a lab. I had stage three breast cancer.

The reality of my situation slowly began to sink in. I had to start treatment right away. Thank goodness for that mammogram! Then I remembered why I got it: Floyd Henry had been trying to alert me to the danger he'd smelled on my breath. He had even tried to show me exactly where the tumor was when he bumped me.

After my first treatment, Floyd Henry greeted me at the door. Like usual, he snorted and huffed at my face. But this time I thanked him. "You're a good boy, Floyd Henry. A good boy, and an angel."

One year of chemotherapy and radiation shrank the tumor so that my surgeon could remove it. Throughout treatment, Floyd Henry was at my side. I've now been cancer-free for more than three years. My tumor was detected in time for treatment—thanks to the newspaper ad I couldn't ignore. We're all put on this earth for a reason. Floyd Henry was put here to save my life.

The Little Red Hen

Josephine M. Kuntz

AT ONE POINT DURING THE winter, my husband, a house painter, was temporarily unemployed because of the weather, and the textile plant where I worked was closed due to a seasonal layoff. We literally had no money. To make matters worse, our eighteen-month-old daughter, Rachel, was recovering poorly from pneumonia, and the doctor insisted we feed her a boiled egg each day. Even that was beyond our means.

"Why not pray for an egg?" suggested our babysitter, who was staying on without pay to help us. We were a churchgoing family, but this teenager's depth of faith was something new to us at the time. All the same, she and I got on our knees and told the Lord that Rachel needed an egg each morning. We left the problem in His hands.

About ten o'clock that morning we heard some cackling coming from the hedge fence in front of our house. There among the bare branches sat a fat red hen. We had no idea where she had come from. We just watched in amazement as she laid an egg and then proceeded down the road, out of sight.

The little red hen that first day was a surprise, and we thanked God for it, but can you imagine how startled we were when we heard the hen cackling in the hedge the next morning? And the morning after that, and the morning after that? Every day for over a week, Rachel had a fresh boiled egg.

Rachel grew better and better, and at last the weather turned and my husband went back to work. The next morning I waited by the window and watched. But our prayers had been answered—precisely.

The little red hen did not come back. Ever.

Underwater Angels

Mary C. Neal, MD

I COMPLETED MY FIRST SCUBA course and became passionate about the sport. I gave up my paychecks and began working in exchange for equipment. When the shop sponsored a trip to the Florida Springs, I couldn't wait to go. The drive from Lexington to Florida was long and our group arrived after dark, but the water was beautiful, calm, and inviting that evening. We novices were so eager to make our first open-water dive that we compelled our instructors to break the first rule of night diving: Never dive at night where you haven't yet dived during the daytime.

We impatiently donned our equipment and enthusiastically jumped into the water. Once under the surface, I stuck to my instructor like glue. We cruised along the bottom and I was thrilled with the splendor of the fish and the variety of the colors and shapes of the coral. My first open-water dive was living up to all of my expectations and, too soon for me, the air in our tanks neared empty and it was time to surface.

When we inflated our vests and kicked toward the surface, we did not pop through the water's surface as expected, but we solidly struck rock. We swam in another direction and again struck rock. We had inadvertently entered a cave to which the exit was not obvious.

My instructor and I searched for the opening, but the visibility had been diminished when, in my inexperience, I kicked the bottom of the lake with my fins and raised a cloud of silt. We were running out of air and the tank alarms were echoing. That's when I remembered to pray. I called out to God and I was immediately filled with the feeling of God's presence and the knowledge that He would show us the way out. He would see me through.

The silt began to clear and we saw several fish darting back and forth before lining up together, swimming in the current. They seemed to beckon us to follow, which we did. We made one last dive down to the bottom of the water in the direction of the fish, then swam upward and broke through the surface of the lake just as my instructor's air tank emptied completely.

My instructor and I discussed our shared experience at length. He was entirely focused on himself, and was distraught at having lost control of the situation. He felt responsible for the mistakes that were made and what he thought was his poor judgment. He believed that we had survived because of pure luck. He judged himself a failure and proceeded to drink himself into a state of oblivion. For my part, I had a profoundly different response to our survival. I did not believe that luck was involved. I had experienced a profound sense of calm and a knowledge that God was with us in the cave. I believed we had survived because God intervened, even though we had been such knuckleheads and He essentially had to push us out of the cave.

No (Large) Dogs Allowed

Sandra Headrick

DAD AND I WERE WALKING through the grounds of his gated senior community when he staggered. "Are you okay?" I asked. Dad just stayed quiet—something was wrong. No one else was in sight. *I have to get Dad back to his house,* I thought. But I didn't have the strength to keep him steady.

Out of nowhere a large tan-and-white dog appeared at my father's side. He must have weighed one hundred pounds. Dad put his hand on the dog's back to steady himself. With the help of that dog we made it home. I got Dad into the backseat of his car and rushed inside to alert Mom and grab the car keys. I stepped back outside and glanced up and down the street, looking for the dog. He was nowhere to be seen. *How did he disappear so quickly?* I wondered.

Dad stayed the night in the hospital. The next morning I went to the management office of Dad's community. "Who owns the big, strong tan-and-white dog?" I asked.

"Large dogs are not permitted here," the manager said. "Not even to visit. It's for safety reasons."

Large dogs weren't allowed. But there were no restrictions on angels.

SPECIAL SECTION

Hark! The Herald Angels Sing!

The Nativity Angel

Kathleen Zarda

AN ANGEL? I GLANCED AT the figurine in my hand, and then at the Nativity set on the coffee table. I had bought this Nativity seven years ago, and I loved setting it up each December. But I'd never noticed an angel in it before. I looked up at the mantel, where I'd placed my collection of angel figurines. *I must have accidentally put one of my angels with the Nativity set when I packed it up last Christmas,* I thought.

But the angel in my hand matched the rest of the Nativity set: same style, same size, same pastel coloring. I placed her in the stable by the sheep.

One week later, Mom passed away. Christmas was hard that year. The following year when I set up the Nativity I looked for the Nativity angel, but she was nowhere to be seen. I counted the figurines. Eleven. *The angel must be the final piece,* I thought. I glanced at the box: 11 PIECE SET.

I counted the pieces again. Three wise men. A shepherd. Jesus, Mary, and Joseph. Four manger animals. There were eleven pieces—but no angel.

A real angel must have known that my first Christmas without Mom would be hard. So she sent a special figurine to watch over my Nativity—and me.

Alight

Jarmila Del Boccio

FROM THE TIME I WAS a young girl, I'd loved hearing stories from the missionaries who visited our church. I dreamed of serving God in a faraway, exotic land one day too. So when I heard of an opportunity to teach a missionary couple's children in the New Guinea bush, I jumped at the chance. I was young and single. In a matter of months I'd quit my job as a nanny, packed up my belongings, and sold my car.

Now I sat alone in the tiny living room of my cabin staring out the window into the pitch-black darkness, a single naked bulb powered by a solar battery the only light. When I imagined life in the bush I hadn't thought about Christmas. "Silent night, holy night…" The tinny sound of my battery-operated tape player seemed to emphasize how alone I was here in a village so primitive, so far from anything I'd ever known. There seemed no way for Christmas to find its way here. How I longed to be home in the Windy City, Michigan Avenue lit with thousands of Italian lights, the glow from the miniature bulbs like angels, snow gently falling from the sky.

Living near the equator, the native people didn't even have a word for cold. I remembered days before trying to teach one of them about snow. I tossed handfuls of packing peanuts into the air. "Snow," I said over and over. He looked at me utterly befuddled. I took him to my minifridge and held his hand against the freezer element. "Hot," he yelled, jumping back in alarm. The concept was beyond the people here.

There had been so many things to adjust to since I'd arrived in July. Nothing could have prepared me for such stark isolation. The missionary couple and their four children were the only people who weren't born in the village. I'd made friends among the two hundred or so native people, but we had little in common. They'd never been to a mall. Or a Cubs game. Never eaten a Chicago deep-dish pizza. Or gazed down from the top of the Sears Tower. It was all as foreign to them as lighting a Christmas tree.

But it was more than that. After dark no one went outside for more than a few minutes, the risk of being bitten by a disease-carrying mosquito too great. And night in the village was dark. No streetlamps, no headlights, no lights in apartment windows. The village, ringed by dense foliage and tall grass, was only accessible to the outside world by plane. It was a two-hour walk one way to the river for water. I felt so trapped, even the ever-temperate climate seemed oppressive.

At home I'd be making sugar cookies right now, I thought. I had learned to eat the local delicacy of roast grasshopper, but that was no treat for Christmas.

My mind went over everything I would be doing back in Chicago, bundled up in my parka. I peered intently into the night, imagining I was outside of Marshall Field's department store, its windows blazing with lights shining down on mechanized Santas and bears, nutcracker soldiers and ballerinas.

That glow. It seemed the very essence of Christmas, the star, the sky filled with angels, the triumph of light over dark. My imagination was no substitute for the real thing.

If anything, inside my cabin, my gloom had only grown. There wasn't even the distant glimmer of a bonfire to break up the darkness. Just a solid black wall. Nothing to do but go to bed. I switched off my tape player. Then the overhead light.

I turned and looked back at the window—

Wow! Just outside my door the night was lit by a cluster of thousands of miniature blinking...Italian Christmas lights? Here? No, these lights were even more beautiful. Breathtaking. Like nothing I'd ever seen in Chicago. I looked closer. They were fireflies. And yet...I'd never seen lightning bugs in New Guinea. God had sent me my very own holiday lighting display—on angel wings! Christmas had come. Just as it had to a tiny, dusty village so many years ago. There were no malls, no crowds of festive shoppers, no tree that first Christmas. Just God's angels announcing the true Light of the world.

Christmas in the Greenhouse

Marilyn Fanning

"POINSETTIAS ARE ORNERY PLANTS," DAD always said, difficult to grow even under the best conditions. Because they preferred the warmth of the Southern sun to the frigid winter temperatures of central New York, Dad watched the weather extra close that time of year and spent a lot of time in the boiler room filling the cavernous furnace with heaps of coal. When the fire was good and hot, the pipes in all nine greenhouses hissed and crackled. They spewed steam that mingled with flower essence and earthen floor to produce a sweet, damp smell. I thought that must be what angels smelled like.

Dad stood outside the house one December day eyeing an ominous sky. "Storm's coming," he said. At twelve years old I hadn't had enough experience to forecast the weather, but I did know his predictions were right. I went with him to the boiler room and checked the coal bin. "Plenty to last us," Dad said. He filled a wheelbarrow and carted it over to the furnace. "Stand back now, Marilyn," he said. He put all of his weight into each throw of the shovel to be sure the coal landed in the fire deep in the back of the furnace. This was backbreaking work, and Dad was strong from doing it. "We got to keep those delicate poinsettias so toasty they have no idea what's going on outside," he said.

By early evening, snow swirled around the greenhouse compound. Our windows at home were so frosty I could barely see out, but every now and then I'd get a whiff of that sweet dampness and know the fire and angels were keeping the poinsettias warm.

Cozy in my bed after dinner I tried to sleep, but the wind rattling the windows woke me more than once. Then, in the dead of night, I heard my father pull on his boots and head out the back door. He always rose at 3:00 AM to do a coaling.

Dad didn't look so good at breakfast. By afternoon he coughed so bad he couldn't take more than a couple of steps before doubling over. After checking his temperature, Mother announced, "It's the grippe, Bill." She forbade him to go out to the greenhouses. "The hired men can get along without you for a day or two," she said, "and I'll see if somebody can stay the night." She made a mustard poultice for Dad's chest, which was about the only flu remedy in those days. At lunchtime, she brought him a bowl of broth and some bread, and delivered some bad news. "We're without help until this storm lets up," Mother said. "The roads are impassable, and it's too dangerous for the men to try to get here on foot."

"But who will coal the boilers?" Dad said. "We'll lose the poinsettias first, then everything will freeze!"

"Marilyn and I will just have to do it," Mother said.

"You can't!" My father coughed out the words. "You don't have the strength."

"We don't have a choice," Mother said. "Marilyn, bundle up."

Fighting our way through the heavy snow, we forced open the door to the boiler room. A full wheelbarrow of coal sat near the furnace. "Now we'll just pray," Mother said, "and God will give us the strength." Then she picked up a shovel. "You grab one, too, and scoop as much coal as you can manage."

Both of us pitched our shovels into the black mound in the wheelbarrow. "You first," Mother said. I swung my shovel back and threw the coal with all my might. It went into the furnace opening—and that was about it. The coal was nowhere near close enough to the fire to do any good. Mother took her turn and grunted when she swung her shovel. But she didn't get much closer than I did.

We stared into the huge cave and at the small fire way in back. It seemed like a hopeless endeavor. "We must keep trying," she said. "Lord, please give us the strength we need." *How is the Lord going to do that?* I asked myself.

When we turned to fill our shovels again, we gasped in fright. A tall, husky man, dirty where he wasn't red from windburn, stood next to the coal bin.

"Maybe I can help," he said.

Mother put her arm protectively around my shoulders. "Where did you come from?" she asked, an edge to her voice.

"Ma'am, it's so cold outdoors, I came in here to get warm." The big man glanced into the furnace. "I can do that job for you," he said.

Practicality got the better of Mother's fear. "I'm sure you can," she said, sounding like my mother again. The man reached for my shovel, and I gladly handed it over. He jabbed it into the pile of coal and wielded that full shovel as if it were light as a feather, throwing right on target. The embers hissed. His next throw got the fire crackling again. Mother and I clapped.

"Our livelihood depends on the fire staying lit," Mother said. "I'd be more than grateful if you'd keep it going overnight, Mister—?"

"John," the man said. "Just John. You can be sure I'll keep it going. This feels like heaven to me."

"Are you hungry?" Mother asked.

"For now, keeping warm is the only thing on my mind." John settled in on a bench near the furnace.

"I'll be back in the morning with some food, and I hope you have a warm night's rest. You can wash up at the sink in the back room if you want," Mother said. "Good night. And thank you!"

Mother and I returned to the house to tell Dad the good news. "Wait till you see this man called John," Mother said. "He's over six feet tall and strong as an ox.

Throws coal as well as you. He wandered into the greenhouse for shelter and I put him to work!"

"God knows I'm willing to help a guy who's down on his luck," Dad said. "But this time we're more helped than helping."

Mother laughed. "When I asked the Lord to send us strength, He did me one better and sent a strapping man to do the job."

By daylight, Mother had fixed a basket with a bowl of hot oatmeal, biscuits and jam, and apples from the fruit cellar. "You carry the towels and soap," she told me.

As we pushed open the greenhouse door, Mother exclaimed, "Oh, it's warm in here. We're going to be all right!"

John was sitting on a bench among the poinsettias and greeted us with a big smile. "Can you work another day?" Mother asked, handing him the basket and coffee. "We'll pay you for your work." John nodded and dug into his breakfast.

That day the storm subsided and Dad's fever broke. "Don't rush out to the greenhouses just yet," Mother said. "John's taking care of the coaling. Let's make sure you're well." She brought John lunch, and then dinner. The furnace was well tended.

"You know," Dad said that night, "maybe I could afford to hire another hand. I feel I owe that man something."

But when Dad dressed the next morning and went to the boiler room, John wasn't there. On the bench, neatly folded, lay the towels. The dinner dishes had been rinsed and stacked in Mother's basket. "John's gone," Dad told us at the house.

"A hobo gone without the pay he was due? How can that be?" Mother asked.

"You said yourself the Lord sent him, Mildred. Maybe there's more truth in that than you realized. All I know is, the good man's gone."

With the storm gone as well, business resumed. The regular workers returned and customers descended on us once more. Christmas was only two weeks away, and that year Dad's poinsettias were more beautiful than ever, the flowers extra large and the leaves a vibrant green. I walked among them, admiring them, the steam hissing and crackling in the pipes, releasing the sweet smell of greenhouse angels.

Christmas Feather

Lorna Byrne

A WOMAN CALLED MAURA TOLD me a lovely story of how the angels had comforted her one Christmas after her husband had died. Maura was at her kitchen sink, washing dishes and remembering the good times when her husband and her children were all together—the birthdays, christenings, but particularly the Christmases. Her children were all grown up now but were still very close to her. She had a wonderful family, but that didn't fill the loneliness of missing the man she had loved dearly. She was feeling so sad and so alone, and there were tears in her eyes as she begged, "Just give me a sign. Show me that you really are there, that you haven't gone away completely."

She followed some instinct and just left the dishes in the sink and walked across the kitchen and out into the garden. The weather was cold and changeable, and she stood there in the cold looking around her, wondering to herself whether her husband could really be in heaven, whether he could still be with her in spirit. She looked at trees and plants that had grown since he had died, and then, out of nowhere it seemed to her, it started to snow.

Maura laughed and, feeling her husband's presence in some way, she spoke to him out loud. "So you have me out in the garden, and now it's starting to snow. I'm freezing and it's snowing." The snowflakes kept falling and then, for no reason she could explain, one falling snowflake attracted her. It was no different from any of the other snowflakes that were falling around her, but she had a very strong urge to catch that particular snowflake. She reached out, and the snowflake landed on her hand. She looked at it in amazement. The snowflake wasn't melting. As she looked more closely, she realized that it wasn't a snowflake. It was a feather, a tiny feather no bigger than a snowflake. There were no birds around. There was nowhere it could have come from. As she touched the feather, tears came into her eyes and she said a heartfelt thank-you. She thanked God and the angels and she thanked her much-loved husband.

Christmas Eve Butterfly

Ann Browning

DOESN'T SEEM RIGHT TO BE here on Christmas Eve, but here we are in a hospital—just Mom and me. She has been ill for several months—cancer and treatments for cancer. Which is worse?

My family has left to spend the holiday with other family members. It was my idea so the kids could have some normalcy where there has been none. The doctor has told us that time is short, that Mom's fever will spike and...

It is so hard to realize what is happening. She has been in and out of consciousness for the last few days, but I know. I feel that these are the last hours. She and I have talked some, but it is hard for her.

The nurses, kind and helpful, have brought me a cot. Lying in the semidarkness, I actually pray for daylight. The sun means a new day, maybe a better day for my mom.

I doze. I awaken. It is that routine for hours. Nurses come and go. Then no one.

I lie here and listen to my mother's ragged breathing, and I pray. Then I doze again. A nurse quietly enters the room and I watch. Nothing is said. She pulls out a stool that's beneath the bed and sits, or seems to. No words. Silence.

I think I may have dozed again, but movement wakens me. The nurse is standing in the doorway—backlit, so I cannot see her face but only her white clothing. And then she speaks to me. "Don't worry. The butterfly is already gone. This is just the old cocoon."

I don't move. I can't. Those words, so gentle, so kind, so appropriate. I glance toward the window and through my tears realize that it is almost dawn. It's Christmas Day.

Soon the hospital begins the new day—nurses in, then the doctor. "No, it doesn't look good. Yes, her fever is up. I don't know how much time." But I know.

I call my family about midmorning, explaining what the doctor has said, but not what I know.

The day is long and hard, hard for everyone. But hardest for my mom. She knows it's Christmas Day, her favorite. She works to stay awake, but her breathing is horrible. Oxygen is given.

The family tells me to leave the hospital for a while, and reluctantly I do. Two hours later: "Come quickly!"

Around 8:00 PM or as I think of it, the end of my mother's day, dishes are washed, leftovers are put away, it's time to relax.

The tears, few words, nothing can be said, not now. My family and I have gathered with friends in another room to await the formalities. And it occurs to me something my mother might say: "All right, now. It's over. Go wash your face and hands. You'll be all right." That's what she would say, always—whether skinned knee or family death.

I leave the room to find the nurse who spoke to me that morning. At the desk, I ask for the duty nurse for my mom around dawn. One nurse looks at me and says, "That was me, but I didn't come in because you and your mother were sleeping, and we had an emergency on the floor. All of us were down there."

As I walk back toward my family, I know. My visitor with the gentle words and kind voice had been the answer to my prayers. Her words soothed my soul and lifted my spirit. She had not come for my mother; she had come to prepare me.

Roadside Rescue

Rosemarie McManus

WRAPPED PRESENTS, HOMEMADE KNIT STOCKINGS, fresh-baked goods—I ran through a mental checklist of all the things I needed to bring to my son's for Christmas Eve. Despite my recently acquired walking cane, I'd wheeled everything from my apartment to the car in a shopping cart. Just because I lived in a retirement community didn't mean I needed help getting ready for Christmas. I slammed shut the trunk. *Ready to hit the road!*

Moving to the retirement community had been a big change, although not as big as when I left Germany for America after World War II. I no longer had space to host Christmas Eve dinner. Fortunately, my son and his family lived nearby and had offered to pick up the torch.

I drove along, smiling at the thought of the young grandchildren's happy faces when they saw all the goodies. On the radio, Bing Crosby sang "White Christmas." Outside, the icy wind howled and the sky was laden with snow clouds, but I felt warmed by the Christmas spirit.

I was a few miles from my son's when the engine made a funny sound. It coughed, sputtered, coughed again. *That doesn't sound good.* I quickly turned the wheel and pulled over to the grassy median on my left. Or tried to. I came to a stop with the rear of the car still sticking out into the fast lane. The gas pedal didn't respond. Then I noticed the glowing orange icon on the dashboard display, and the gas tank needle. Empty.

How could I have neglected to keep an eye on my gas gauge? Me, who didn't need any help? Why hadn't I listened to my children's pleas to get a cell phone?

"*Mein heilig Schutzengel,*" I prayed in German. *Angel of God, my guardian dear.* Cars honked. Drivers were impatient to get where they were going. I got out to flag someone down. Someone slowed to warn me to get out of traffic. Another, irate, yelled, "Call the cops!" Everyone else zoomed by at sixty miles per hour.

I stood there, leaning on my cane, shaking with cold and fear, almost in tears. The sky was getting dark. *They'll be wondering where I am.* Could I walk to a service station? I'd have to cross the four-lane highway at the very least. *What do I do?*

Just then, a gray compact car pulled up. A man behind the wheel, a woman in the passenger seat. The woman got out and hurried toward me. She was of medium height, roundly built, her oval face framed by dark, wavy hair. She seemed to shimmer, surrounded with an aura of light. Before I could say a word about my predicament, she called to me. "Go back and sit in your car. We've come to help you."

"Oh, thank you! Thank you!" I shouted. I did as she told me.

She came to my window. "You'll be all right," she said. "We'll get enough gas for you to drive to a station."

I watched the gray car drive off. After a minute, it returned, and the woman stepped out carrying a red gas can. She opened my gas cap and poured.

"How can I thank you?" I called to her. "Let me pay you for the gas."

She shook her head.

"You're like my guardian angel this Christmas Eve," I said.

She laughed, finished pouring, and handed me the empty gas can. "Here, keep this in your trunk. Someday you can help someone else." Then she leaned in the window and gave me a feather-light hug. "Merry Christmas. We'll watch out for you as you pull back into traffic."

I guessed everyone needed help some time, old and young alike. I started the engine and pulled into the lane. "I'm okay!" I called out, and looked back to wave good-bye.

Only the gray car was gone. That's when I wondered. *How did they know gas was what I needed?* I'd never told them.

Christmas Lists Come True

Suzy Zabel

WHEN MY HUSBAND OF TWELVE YEARS walked out on me and our two young children, I didn't know how we would survive. I made little at my cleaning and haircutting jobs, and we couldn't afford to stay in our home. We packed up and drove to Idaho, where relatives helped us find a small house for rent.

Then the holidays arrived. The kids approached me with puppy-dog eyes. "Mom, can we go to the mall? Santa's there!" *Sure, why not,* I figured. They made out their Christmas lists. A trendy doll for Katiebeth. A big Lego set for Keith. New clothes for both. *Nothing I can afford,* I worried.

The kids lined up and finally got their turn on Santa's knee. Afterward, they seemed so excited. How could I let them down? At a thrift store, I found some passable used clothes, books, a board game. I wrapped and hid the gifts in the closet. *Lord, please help the kids understand.*

Christmas Eve, it snowed all day. I was getting the kids to bed when our doorbell rang. Who would visit so late? I peered through the peephole. A snow-covered Santa held a big black bag.

"Ho, ho, ho, merry Christmas!" he said. The kids ran to the door and shrieked with delight. "Have you been good?" he asked. They nodded.

Santa reached into his bag. Out came a doll for Katie. A Lego set for Keith. And brand-new clothes, in the kids' sizes. My arms held a pile of pants and shirts and dresses!

I stood in stunned silence as Santa turned to go, shutting the door behind him. "Wait!" I called. I put the clothes down and pulled the door back open.

Santa was nowhere to be seen. Not even his boot print on our snow-covered front yard.

Tow Truck Angel

Joan Wester Anderson

CHRISTINE MUHLBAUER'S POSTAL SERVICE SHIFT ended about three o'clock on Christmas Eve morning. Despite the freezing cold, she decided to stop at the all-night grocery store on her way home to buy ingredients for Christmas cookies. "My family calls me 'The Christmas Kid,'" Christine says. "I am really into the season and love making cookies." When she came out with her packages, however, she found that she had run over some broken glass in the parking lot. She inspected her tires and they looked fine and she decided to drive home.

But the car lurched and rattled, and the steering wheel jumped in her hands. She had no cell phone to call anyone and began asking the angels for protection. Slipping and sliding, she pulled over to the side of the road, got out, and then she noticed. A flat tire. *It's going to be one of those nights,* she thought and walked the rest of the way to a lighted diner not too far up the road.

"When I got there, I pulled out my wallet, which had the phone number of Jessie, my regular mechanic's towing service," she says. "A woman answered the phone and took the information down and told me to hold on. A man's voice came over the phone next and he asked me to repeat my location and said he would be there as soon as possible." In the meantime, a patrol car had pulled up at the diner. The patrolman walked in, wondering about Christine's car, which she had left on the shoulder of the road, with the flashers on. "I told him it was my car and that I was getting a tow truck," she says. "He made sure that I was confident that help was coming and then left."

All routine so far. She would be home soon, Christie reassured herself. Soon a bright blue unmarked truck pulled up. Christine went out to meet the driver and get into the truck. "He wore a shaggy beard, and jeans, and spoke quietly," she says. "I did think it strange that there was no name or markings on the truck, but I somehow knew he had been sent to me. We drove back to my car on the shoulder, he hitched it up, and we agreed he would tow it to my mechanic, Jessie."

But Jessie's garage was locked, the lot empty and deserted. Christine watched as the tow truck driver calmly wrote a note of explanation and stuck it through the key drop. "All set," he told Christine. "Would you like a ride home now?"

"I sure would," Christine said. It had been a long night, but everything had worked out. Even the tow truck driver, although quiet, was a reassuring presence. Christine felt certain she had met him before, but her foggy brain was too tired to think about it. "How much is the tow?" she asked, as they pulled into her driveway.

"Oh, work it out with Jessie," he said.

Christine got out, but before she could muster up some words of thanks, the truck pulled away. "I honestly didn't see exactly where it went," Christine says. "It seemed to vanish into thin air, but I knew such a thing couldn't happen."

The next day Christine got a ride to Jessie's garage, and she described the truck. "Did he charge you for the tow?" Jessie asked, a puzzled expression on his face.

"No," Christine told him. "He said to work it out with you."

"I don't do it that way," Jessie responded. "My tow driver, Pat, and I have a standing arrangement. But Pat's truck is orange, and it says 'Pat's Towing' on the side."

He called Pat and was surprised to learn that Pat hadn't had any emergency calls the night before.

"But I dialed your number," Christine pointed out, showing Jessie the card she used, "and a woman answered and then put a man on the phone, who then came out to get me in a bright blue truck...."

"Impossible," Pat insisted. "I didn't pick anyone up last night."

"Well," Jessie looked at Christine's tire, by now ripped to shreds, "*someone* had to tow you because you couldn't have driven the car in that condition."

"Didn't the driver leave his name on the note?" Christine asked, extremely mystified.

"What note?" Jessie asked.

"The note he put through your key drop."

Jessie looked at Christine. "There was no note left for me, there or anywhere."

"But I saw him drop it...." Christine described the driver, slender with shaggy hair....

"That's not Pat," Jessie interrupted. "He's big and bald."

The two looked at each other. "Jessie wished me a merry Christmas and I wished him the same and left to attend the noon mass at my parish, St. Patrick's," Christine goes on.

"Parishioners were setting up the Christmas crèche before mass, including the life-sized statues." Christine paused to watch for a moment, staring at Balthazar, one of the wise men waiting off in a corner. There was a definite air of familiarity about him, almost as if she knew him.... Shaggy hair, beard... but the statue was made of porcelain, and how could this be? She looked again at the gentle expression on Balthazar. Was that a small smile? Were his eyes meeting hers? Her pastor went over to see what the trouble was.

But there was no trouble, none at all. As Christine explained to the pastor and other helpers, she had thought the tow truck driver was kinder than most.

Now she knew why. "Christmas is a special time," her pastor reminded the group. "Anything can happen."

Christine continues to bake her very best Christmas cookies, for her family and friends, and for a certain truck driver. Was he an angel? A wise man? Who could be sure? But his gentle presence had put the finishing touch on this special night, and Christine will never forget.

Autumn's Christmas Bear

Carol Lee Hughes

AUTUMN GRACE CAME TO US late in life, in January 1993, when Ted and I were facing the empty-nest years, with four older children married or away at college. We didn't know what to expect, starting over with a baby again. But how quickly we fell into the routines of early parenthood, juggling schedules of who had to be where when. Ted's hours as an engineer were reasonably steady, and I had cut back on my courses at a regional campus of the University of Wisconsin, where I was a professor of language arts. Our home was in Oak Creek, Wisconsin, and I'd found a wonderful babysitter who lived on the way to work.

In the blink of an eye, our sleepy newborn grew into an inquisitive toddler. She followed me around the house like a curious duckling, getting into everything. Only one thing could keep her still. Books. Autumn had her favorites—*Carl's Christmas* and *Goodnight, Moon*—and I had mine. We read them all. *The Polar Express* was way beyond her comprehension, but she listened to every word. It must have been my enthusiastic delivery. I was amazed when she began to pick out letters, especially capital *A*. "For 'Autumn,'" we said together.

One chilly winter evening we curled up on the couch to read. "*Mooooon*," Autumn cooed at the big, round face in the blue sky, picking the book she wanted to read first. Next came the one about a rottweiler named Carl. Somehow Carl reminded her of our mixed-breed Labrador, Orion. Autumn planted her chubby little index finger on Carl's hefty figure, calling him Orion before I turned each page.

If Autumn was going to be a lifelong reader, to have the world opened up to her through the written word, I had to let her fall in love with books on her own. I lined up books on low shelves around the house, stuck them under the bedroom dresser, even put some in a bottom kitchen cabinet, places where Autumn could discover them herself. There were always books within her reach, and she often plunked herself down on the floor to "read" one. Poring over the pages, she played the part of serious student. And then one day I heard her, in a mixture of babbling and recognizable two- and three-word phrases, mimicking the pauses and intonations of expressive reading. She was developing her own reading voice!

As winter deepened, Ted, Autumn, and I spent more time in front of the fireplace, Autumn in her wooden rocker, holding her stuffed Christmas bear. Ever since her grandmother had given it to her, on her very first Christmas, Autumn hadn't spent a night without that bear. She loved it. When she pressed its paw a hidden computer chip played music. Sometimes Autumn pressed the paw once too often and I hoped I'd never hear the carols it played again. Autumn's second Christmas had passed, but I knew there was no chance of her letting me put the bear away until next year.

Only days after her second birthday, on January 31, 1995, Autumn and I were driving to her babysitter's when we were in a car accident. I don't remember the crash itself, but I was aware enough to know that ambulance attendants were loading me into a Flight for Life. They were not loading my daughter.

Ted got to the hospital while I was being prepped for surgery. "Autumn...," I whispered. Ted held me tight. "The ambulance has arrived," he said. "We can hold her."

We cradled our little girl, hugging her gently, telling her good-bye, though we knew she was already gone.

From a hospital bed, winter seemed even harsher. My operation, the pain, the physical therapy, even the signs of healing—all pointed to the awful fact that I was alive while my daughter, who had been in my care, was not. I spent hours staring out the window at a cruel and capricious world. *Why, God?* I finally asked one day, the question breaking a dam of grief and anger. *Why did You give us Autumn only to snatch her away? Where was her guardian angel while mine saved me? Or aren't angels real at all?*

Just then Ted walked in. I wasn't much for making conversation those days, and there weren't words for my sadness anyway. Ted seemed to accept my silence. He came and sat beside me on the bed.

"I'm not going to get well," I told him. "Even if I could, I wouldn't."

My husband studied my eyes as if he were trying to see our future in them. He looked so tired. "Carol Lee, if you don't make it through this, I won't either."

Ted was careful with his words; he didn't say things unless he truly meant them. For the first time since the accident I felt something besides my own pain: I was sad for him too. "I'm so sorry, Ted. You lost Autumn too. We'll get through this together."

I went to God to ask for strength. It was a relief to pray without anger and bitterness, to open myself to His graces. I also tried to put words to my sadness. Writing had always been a kind of therapy for me. Maybe it could help me now. I wrote a poem with the line: "No life so small that it cannot change the world." After that, the questions I brought to God took a different turn: *How did Autumn's life make a difference? How can it continue to make a difference?*

Shuffling around my bedroom after I got home from the hospital, I accidentally knocked over a pile of Autumn's books. I wanted to leave evidence of Autumn scattered around the house—her books, her wooden rocker, her Christmas bear.

I would never let her disappear from our lives. Holding her favorite, *Goodnight, Moon*, I wondered, *How can Autumn touch other lives too?*

I went to the phone and dialed information. "Children's Hospital of Wisconsin," I requested. There was only one children's hospital in the entire state, and it happened to be in Milwaukee, adjacent to the hospital where Autumn and I had been taken.

"Do you have any permanent provision for buying books?" I asked the children's support director, who took my call.

"I'm afraid not," she said. "Cutbacks have hit us hard, and buying medical equipment comes first. It's a shame, though."

That night I talked to Ted. "If Autumn had been able to recover in the hospital," I told him, "we both know what she would have spent most of her time doing." And that was the start of the Autumn Grace Hughes Fund, to provide hospitalized youngsters with books. We let family and friends know how they could help keep Autumn's spirit alive. Donations came in, some as small as fifty cents. Months passed, and the fund grew as word of our mission spread. I put in our first order at the local bookstore. We had bookplates made with a photo of Autumn reading, taken just weeks before her death.

Already it had been nearly a year since that awful day. I still had dark moments when my faith wavered and I asked the hard questions all over again. Was there a loving God? Had I started this fund to help other children, or was it a desperate way to hang on to my own child? In the end I always chose to believe that there were messengers between heaven and earth, that Autumn was alive with God, and that she'd be very pleased to share her love of books with other children. I had to believe.

Deep inside, though, I wished I knew.

One day in mid-December I'd arranged to drop off the very first donations from the fund. The snowy night before, Orion and I were the only ones home. I let our dog in, and started a fire while he shook himself off by the door. "There, now," I said, gazing into the flames, "this'll warm us up."

Autumn had always been mesmerized by our fires. This was the first one built since she'd died. Ted had put her little wooden rocker a safe distance from the crackling embers. Now her Christmas bear sat there looking on. I straightened the bear's hat and smoothed its sweatshirt. The chair continued to rock for a moment after my fussing. I would have given anything for Autumn to squeeze that bear paw and start the music. I couldn't even remember which carols it played. I had to smile, remembering how attached Autumn had been to that bear, and I went up to bed with happy thoughts of her.

I awoke the next morning feeling different. Gone was the sadness that dulled most of my days since Autumn had died. I passed over the drab clothes I'd been wearing all year, and reached in the back of my closet for a skirt with bright snow-flakes on it. "Today," I told myself, "is my Christmas day." I dressed and went downstairs.

There on the table, in neat stacks, were brand-new hardback copies of *The Polar Express*, *The Littlest Angel*, *Carl's Christmas*, and *Goodnight, Moon*. All ready for the children at the hospital. I checked the envelope holding the book-plates and hoped we had enough. Then I heard Orion scratching to be let in.

"Cold out there, boy?" I asked, opening the back door. Orion stepped inside and, fastidious as usual, stood on the mat shaking himself off and cleaning the snow from his paws. I remembered I'd left the chimney flue open and crossed the room to the hearth. As I leaned into the fireplace to pull the flue, I heard it. Distinctly. Music. A Christmas carol, "The First Noel."

I turned, stunned.

On the little wooden rocker Autumn's Christmas bear sat perfectly still, the chair motionless. The bear was playing a carol.

But who had pressed its paw?

"The angel did say..." came the bear's song.

I looked over at Orion, who hadn't moved from the back door. No one else was in the house. The carol played through, and the music stopped.

Finally I knew. I didn't have the answers to all my hard questions, but I knew for sure that angels are real. Sometimes God sends them to help us accept life's tragedies and find a way to make good come of them. Autumn was alive with God in heaven, and her short life on earth would continue to make a difference. With new purpose, I picked up the books and headed for the door. The children were waiting.

Wings of Love

Cheryl Johnston

A MONTH AFTER MY MOTHER died, depression stalked me.

Normally, I'm one of those upbeat, see-the-good-in-all-things, blessings-overflowing types. My childhood home was filled with laughter, and until I was twelve, my father sang encouraging songs to me like "You Are My Sunshine" and "Let the Sunshine In." Even today, my husband, RJ, lovingly calls me Pollyanna.

From my earliest memories I was aware of my mother's faith. Her parents were evangelists, and the Michigan church they eventually established is now more than eighty years old. Five of their seven children became preachers.

At age fourteen, Mom's world shattered when her beloved mother died. Desperation triggered knee-jerk decisions that took her to California, away from family and faith and into two divorces by age nineteen. She longed for someone to fill the hole in her heart.

The next year, Dorcas Roberta Spooner married Robert Vernon Christensen and they vowed, "'Til death do us part."

Five years later, I was born and by my parents' seventh anniversary, along came the twins, Peggy and Paula. Like all young families, ours juggled finances, but overall life was good and we were happy...that is until diabetes took Daddy from us too soon at forty-two.

At his funeral, I remember seeing my strong and independent thirty-seven-year-old mother crumble. I watched her sink into despair, fearful of our future.

Many mornings, Paula, Peggy, and I would wake to discover our tiny, working mother had fallen asleep with an open Bible across her chest. And many nights we'd seen her on her knees, praying.

For the rest of her life, she relied on God.

Mom had always loved holidays, especially Christmas. She tried to make things special for her three, with Norman Rockwell touches like trinket-filled stockings, new pajamas with slipper socks, the traditional turkey dinner, and several extraspecial presents she had somehow found the money to afford.

She delighted in driving us through neighborhood lighted Christmas displays. We looked forward also to the local Christmas productions at nearby churches. And in the house where she lived alone in her later years, she played piano and sang Christmas carols just for her own and God's enjoyment.

Seven days before Mom's death at age seventy, our extended family had shared a beautiful but bittersweet Thanksgiving. Everyone gathered at Paula's to share the turkey dinner, family game time, and catch-up conversations. By evening it was evident Mom was struggling to smile. The lung cancer she'd been battling the past year had invaded her stomach and brain. On this night it had sapped her stamina, and dark circles underlined her eyes.

Looking back, I think she knew, but little did we suspect that within the week, Jesus would welcome her home.

My sad state then, a few weeks afterward on the morning of December 22, was simply a selfish one—I missed her. In those weeks after her funeral, I hadn't wanted to dress or eat or even step outside. My interest in celebrating Christmas was zero. There were no gift-wrapped packages or decorated tree or anything to make our home holiday-ready.

Sitting alone in the dark house, I couldn't shake the grief and depression that overwhelmed me. Sobbing uncontrollably, I called a dear friend for help. When she heard the deep anguish in my voice, she began to pray. Her petition was powerful and pleading. She begged God to calm my spirit and comfort me, to cover and enfold me. She asked that I would feel His love and presence in a palpable way.

Her prayer worked.

Even though my heart wasn't in it, by day's end I had managed to purchase and wrap gifts for RJ, our grandbabies, our sons, and their wives.

By ten that evening, I was relaxed but exhausted when I fell into bed, my eyes still swollen from tears. Thoughts and sweet memories of my mother cradled my deep sleep.

Suddenly, I was awake, still on my back with eyes opened wide, to stare at the bedroom's vaulted ceiling.

On the dresser to the right, the digital alarm clock's red numerals displayed 2:45.

Then, from the left I heard a noise and shifted my stare toward the sliding glass door on the room's western wall.

On the valance rod above the door was perched a large white bird.

Thinking my eyes were playing tricks on me, I used thumbs and forefingers to pry them open even more.

Sure enough, there it was, a white bird—posed, as if on a mission.

With one quick swoosh of its wings, it swooped down and hovered over the bed, startling me. My arms flailed as I clutched the sheets and tried to wake RJ. The bird's wings sounded like rushing, whispered wind. My chest heaved in anticipation—not in fear, but in awe. The bird pronounced one word, slowly and with authority. *"Peace!"*

I sensed it didn't want me to disturb my husband's sleep. As the wings fluttered gracefully, the bird spoke again. *"Peace! This is for Cheryl. Your mother is in heaven."*

I remember my heart leaping inside my chest as I panted for breath. I remember realizing the bird was actually a dove. I remember understanding this message was meant only for me. I remember staring, amazed at the experience. And I remember feeling infinitely loved as I drifted back into sleep. When I awoke later that morning from one of my best rests ever, RJ asked, "What went on in here last night?"

I started to explain, but his disbelieving laughter sealed my lips. But I know. And whether or not anyone else believes what I saw, I know. The dove's words offered an absolute assurance that changed my life—the peace that forever passes all understanding.

Angel on a Ladder

Delores E. Topliff

CONNIE MET LARRY AT A church garage sale he was helping set up. Excited about the creative writing class she was attending in my home, she mentioned it to Larry and sparked his interest. He's a devoted family man and marathon runner who does home repairs and remodeling with a craftsman's heart.

But he'd also written his first fun unpublished children's book, *Henry, the Kite,* which he'd illustrated with professional-quality color art. Connie suggested Larry join our writing class, and he did.

Loving what Larry had already written, I challenged him to draft a second story—and then a third. Looking around my townhome he quietly suggested swapping skills hour for hour. Instead of paying me for writing instruction or editing, he offered his skills in my home. He soon installed updated lighting in my kitchen and bathroom, and suggested other improvements.

But job demands cut back Larry's writing time. We exchanged encouraging e-mails while summer found him busier still.

In November, my pastor announced that church young people would cook Thanksgiving dinner and do home or car repairs for widows. I thought, *Splendid.* But my second thought hurt. *Lord, in every way except legally, I'm a widow. My children's father left when our boys were three years and sixteen months and hasn't been in our lives since—but the church doesn't realize that.*

Larry sent another e-mail. He'd worked more on his second story and started illustrations. He'd brainstormed a third book and wanted input. Would I take a look?

Yes.

When he came, I loved Larry's perky art and great progress with characters and plot. "My offer still stands," he said, smiling while looking around my house. "You must have some home projects you want done."

I hesitated. I'd lived in this home nine years but hadn't repainted the walls. Except for my grandchildren's fingerprint smudges, the walls weren't terrible. But the uninviting institutional white did nothing for us. I longed to introduce color, even phoned my talented decorator sister in Oregon for suggestions.

But painting would be too much to ask Larry, wouldn't it? The time required would be way more than anything he needed for writing instruction or editing. "Will you accept time plus payment?"

"No," he answered. "Your time's invaluable to me. An investment toward my writing. Plus if you say the occasional prayer for my family—that would be wonderful and make us more than even."

I turned away before Larry saw my tears. He checked his pocket calendar. "I could paint the week before Christmas. Most clients don't want their homes torn up then, but if you wouldn't mind…"

"That works for me."

"Great. What color do you want?"

"I'm considering—even prayed about it…"

"And?"

I showed him several paint chip samples, but my eyes kept returning to the string of creamy peach freshwater pearls I'd bought back from a mission trip to the Philippines. "That's the color," the Lord seemed to whisper.

Larry met me at the paint store and helped me match my pearls to a color sample. We bought quality supplies at discount and he came the next morning with ladder and scaffolding. For most of three days he cheerfully brightened my rooms with fresh color and great attention to detail. While he painted, we shared inspiring stories. Again and again, some trick of late December sunlight turned his athletic form on the ladder into the shadow of an angel moving across my stairwell and walls. A tall winged angel sweeping its wings in blessing.

That image remains. Larry finished painting before Christmas and it was my best Christmas present ever. And every day since I enjoy clean walls with warm color while seeing images of a tall strong angel with wings sweeping across my walls, blessing me and my loved ones with kindness beyond anything I could have imagined.

Though I didn't fit the usual definition of a widow, God provided something better. Glowing paint and a cheerful lingering, brightening presence that warms my home every day.

To Our Readers

Conari Press, an imprint of Red Wheel/Weiser, publishes books on topics ranging from spirituality, personal growth, and relationships to women's issues, parenting, and social issues. Our mission is to publish quality books that will make a difference in people's lives—how we feel about ourselves and how we relate to one another. We value integrity, compassion, and receptivity, both in the books we publish and in the way we do business.

Our readers are our most important resource, and we appreciate your input, suggestions, and ideas about what you would like to see published.

Visit our website at *www.redwheelweiser.com* to learn about our upcoming books and free downloads, and be sure to go to *www.redwheelweiser.com/newsletter* to sign up for newsletters and exclusive offers.

You can also contact us at *info@rwwbooks.com*.

Conari Press
an imprint of Red Wheel/Weiser, LLC
65 Parker Street, Suite 7
Newburyport, MA 01950
www.redwheelweiser.com